THE LOCKHEED F-117 *NIGHTHA*

The first F-117A, No. 780, during the course of pre-first-flight check-out. Static engine runs like this were conducted inside Groom Lake hangar to maintain security.

Full-scale F-117 wood mock-up under construction during late 1979 inside Building 309/310 at Burbank Plant B-6. At the time, the program was codenamed Senior Trend.

CREDITS:

This booklet is the result of contributions and efforts made on behalf of the author and Aerofax, Inc. by the following individuals: John Andrews of Testor Corp., Capt. Kevin Baggetti, Michael Binder, Kearney Bothwell of Hughes, Tom Copeland, Greg Fieser, Rene' Francillon, Charles Fleming, Jim Goodall, Lt. Eric Holman, E.S. "Mule" Holmberg, Bob Johnson, John Kerr, Tony Landis, Capt. Greg Meland, Steven Miller of the 37th TFW, Scott Newman, Dick Pawloski, Chris Pocock, Ralph Poznecki, Ben Rich, Mick Roth, Robert Salvucci of GE Aircraft Engines, Bobby Shelton of the 37th TFW, Richard Stadler of Lockheed, Jim Stevenson, Bill Sweetman, Katsuhiko Tokunaga, Deborah Vito of Schubert & Company, Barbara Wasson, and Dwight Weber of General Electric.

INTRODUCTION:

This is the second revised edition of Aerofax's Extra describing Lockheed Martin's F-117 *Nighthawk*. It is the result of many different events, not the least of which was the success of the airplane in the Middle East and its associated extensive use in *Operation Desert Storm*. Additionally, and as importantly, a considerable body of new information has surfaced via a variety of sources, official and otherwise, that demand an expansive update. Those factors, and the continuing use of the aircraft by the Air Force for the foreseeable future, are the justification for this new edition.

As noted in previous editions, this book has been assembled with only one purpose in mind...to provide the many curious among us with detailed photographic and textual insight into one of the most interesting flying machines of the past several decades— Lockheed's unique F-117 stealth fighter. The timing is purposefully close on the heels of the Department of Defense's longdelayed, but finally consummated decision, during early 1990, to release, within the constraints of security, as much information as possible concerning the F-117 and its mission objectives. Though much remains to be said about this aircraft, and considerably more will be released or leaked during the months and years ahead, this book represents a comprehensive summary to date, with considerable previously unpublished in formation and photography.

COUNTERING RADAR:

It is, of course, the military applications of radar that concern us in this book. Because of radar's extreme importance in locating targets for destruction, extraordinary emphasis has been placed on its development and utilization as well as devices capable of overcoming or countering its capabilities. The latter, in effect, is what the F-117 is all about. Its design has been optimized to create the smallest radar target possible. Coupled with other stealth characteristics described later, it is a second-generation attempt to develop an aircraft that is virtually impossible to track by radar in a combat scenario.

Basically, radar countering techniques (generally referred to as electronic counter-measures or ECM) which now are readily found on virtually all operational combat aircraft and also are applicable to other military hardware as well, can be divided into two broad but basic categories—passive and active. The former involves the utilization of the physical characteristics of the aircraft to mask, within limits, its actual visibility, radar cross-section, active emissions (electronic, infrared, and otherwise), and any other aspect that would reveal its presence to an enemy; and the latter involves the use of systems that actively jam, deceive, or in any other way physically inhibit the enemy's ability to locate and destroy its target via electronic means. When combined, the two disciplines usually are referred to as defensive electronic counter-measures (DECM).

Granted that the objective is to interfere with an enemy's air defense system by inhibiting its sensors, there are basically three options:

1. Radiate active signals optimized to interfere with the enemy's radar.
2. Change the electrical properties of the

Colored flow patterns are visible on low speed oil tunnel model of F-117.

medium through which the radar's energy is being transmitted (usually the atmosphere).

3. Change the reflective properties of the aircraft itself.

The first of these encompasses most jamming and deception systems; the second includes devices such as chaff and absorbing aerosols; and the last includes technologies involving the basic design of the actual vehicle, RAM, and various types of echo distortion systems such as corner reflectors. A description of each follows:

1. Jammers can work in two ways—either by relying on brute force to overwhelm the hostile radar, or by confusing its accuracy. Some dual mode systems can do both. Types include:

(a) Noise jammers take the easy way out and

Operational F-117A, No. 796, off the coast of California. Noteworthy is extended dorsal VHF antenna. This unit, when aircraft is operating in stealth mode, is normally kept in retracted position.

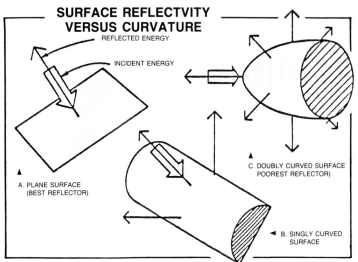

SURFACE REFLECTVITY VERSUS CURVATURE

REFLECTED ENERGY

INCIDENT ENERGY

A. PLANE SURFACE (BEST REFLECTOR)

B. SINGLY CURVED SURFACE

C. DOUBLY CURVED SURFACE POOREST REFLECTOR)

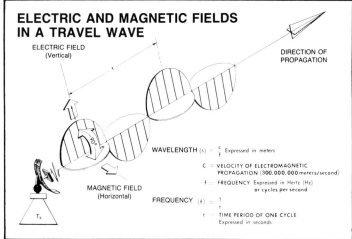

ELECTRIC AND MAGNETIC FIELDS IN A TRAVEL WAVE

ELECTRIC FIELD (Vertical)

DIRECTION OF PROPAGATION

MAGNETIC FIELD (Horizontal)

Tx

WAVELENGTH $(\lambda) = \frac{c}{f}$ Expressed in meters

C = VELOCITY OF ELECTROMAGNETIC PROPAGATION (300,000,000 meters/second)

f = FREQUENCY Expressed in Hertz (Hz) or cycles per second

FREQUENCY $(f) = \frac{1}{t}$

t = TIME PERIOD OF ONE CYCLE Expressed in seconds

Randy Jolly

F-117A, 828, with open drag chute compartment between and just ahead of the vertical tail surfaces. Black coloring and radar absorbing paint is in keeping with low observables philosophy.

MAGNETRON

RESONANT CAVITIES

CATHODE

ANODE

ELECTRONS SPIRALING OUT IN CYCLOIDAL PATH

OUTPUT PROBE

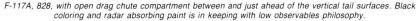

attempt to drown the radar return from the target in an ocean of noise. Noise jamming has many advantages. Relatively few electronic intelligence data are required, and the ECM device will affect anything operating on the frequencies being jammed. The design techniques are simple since the ECM is merely out-shouting the hostile radar. Unfortunately some of the methods for countering noise jammers are equally as simple. The most obvious is to use frequency diversity (or "hopping") and to have a number of different radar frequencies on which to transmit.

(b) Spot noise jamming is the easiest method. A noise-modulated transmitter is set to operate on the frequency of the hostile emitter. This can be countered by enemy equipment fitted with a choice of operating frequencies.

(c) Swept-spot noise jammers continuously scan a range of operating frequencies, interfering with each in turn. As long as all operating frequencies are covered, the threat radar will be regularly disrupted.

(d) Barrage jammers are much simpler, radiating noise over the entire range of frequencies being covered, but for the same effect they need to be more powerful than spot jammers. Such equipment tends to be heavier than spot jammers, as well, but this is offset partially by the need for the latter to carry set-on receivers.

(e) Deception jammers are more complex than the noise generators described above and are based largely on the repeater principle, receiving the hostile signal then re-transmitting it in modified or delayed form (in such a way that the radar thinks it is seeing an echo from another aircraft with a different position or velocity). Surveillance radars build up a picture of the surrounding airspace but tracking radars must concentrate on

a single target. This normally is done by a process known as gating. Once a target has been selected, a tracking radar does not listen continuously between output pulses from the target echo but only at around the time when the echo is expected. It thus is not confused by other targets nearer or further away from its antenna. As the target increases or decreases in range, the gate is moved accordingly. The interval of time between the radar output pulse being transmitted and the gated reply being received is used to measure target range. The gate effectively straddles the return signal within the radar receiver circuitry and is "smart" enough to move in time with the return. Signals outside the gate are simply ignored. Typical deception techniques utilized by these jammers include range-gate pull off, velocity track breaking, inverse amplitude modulation, inverse gain jamming, false target generation, buddy mode (using two aircraft), and cross eye (similar to buddy mode, but utilizing one aircraft with widely separated jamming system antennas).

2. There are basically two ways to change the electrical properties of the medium through which the radar's energy is being transmitted. The most common is via the use of small metallic strips called chaff (during World War II, chaff was referred to as "window") which work by affecting the propogation characteristics of the atmosphere, and the least common is through the very rare use of aerosols which contain metallic particulates.

Chaff operates against radar by creating and/or concealing targets, thereby creating confusion and delay. Chaff is used to assist aircraft in penetrating a radar network undetected and unidentified by creating a multitude of misleading targets or a large area of solid radar returns to confuse and mislead radar operators. Furthermore, even

though the radar may locate the target, the addition of chaff induces errors in tracking radars and may disrupt tracking entirely. Chaff tends to saturate the capability of a radar and to create doubts, confusion, and hesitation among ground radar operators.

When first utilized during WWII against axis radar systems, chaff consisted of thin strips of aluminum foil with a length that was approximately half the wavelength of the radar being countered (today it is known that multiples of one-half the wavelength of the radar signal are suitable; this maximizes the sympathetic electrical resonance effect). The strips were purposefully made thin and light to enhance their ability to float in the atmosphere. Contemporary chaff is generally made of glass or plastic fiber material with a thin metallic film deposited on its surface. The lower density of these base materials enhances "float" characteristics.

Chaff is dispensed in bundles or by machines that can provide strips of varying length in response to the immediate radar threat. For use against low-frequency radars (50 to 100 MHz), lengths of 5 to 10 ft. are common; lower frequency systems, such as those operated by the Germans during World War II, sometimes required chaff strips with lengths of 100 ft. or more.

3. By changing the reflective properties of the aircraft itself, the aircraft's radar cross-section can be modified to a startlingly great degree. It is, in fact, this specific technology that is the essence of the Lockheed F-117's passive defensive system.

Work on materials that absorb, rather than reflect electromagnetic energy first was undertaken successfully by the Germans during World War II. The ability of allied aircraft-borne ASV (air-

Drag chute of F-117A, 84-0828, in fully inflated condition. Noteworthy in this view are the taxi lights. There is a single light attached to each gear strut. Triple-redundancy is the end product of the heavy emphasis being placed on operating the aircraft in total darkness.

to-surface-vessel) radar systems to pick up German submarine snorkels had proven a major frustration, and as a result, a rubberized radar absorbent material (RAM) was developed under a program referred to as *Schornfeinsteger* (Chimneysweep). This proved a modestly effective method of lowering the radar return from the snorkels, but it was far from foolproof—good radar operators often still could find the recharging submarines without significant difficulty.

Regardless, German RAM technology also was applied to other hardware including their aircraft. The most notable of the latter was the stunningly attractive Horten Ho IX. This tailless twin-jet fighter project, perhaps the most advanced in the world at the time of its debut during 1944, was of primarily wood construction (with steel tube framing). Abbreviated test flights were conducted during January of 1945, and were followed by an order for twenty production samples under the designation Gotha Go 229.

Unknown to all but a few, the Gotha variant of the Ho IX also was to become the first viable aircraft designed from the start to incorporate RAM. Though the three Horton Ho IX prototypes (one of which was an unpowered glider) had been built without it, the projected production aircraft would have utilized a wood-laminate skin consisting of two thin plastic-impregnated plywood sheets and a core material made of a sawdust, charcoal, and glue matrix. The latter, optimized to absorb radio energy with minimal return, was crude, but when coupled with the general construction materials of the rest of the aircraft, nevertheless contributed to what almost certainly would have been a very low radar cross section (RCS—i.e., the target's reflectivity in total).

Digressing for a moment, it should be noted that four basic factors determine the amount of reflected energy a radar will receive from a target during any one period of time that the antenna beam is trained on it: (1) the average power—rate of flow of energy—of the radio waves radiated in the target's direction; (2) the fraction of the wave's power which is intercepted by the target and scattered back in the radar's direction; (3) the fraction of that power which is captured by the radar antenna; and (4) the length of time the antenna beam is trained on the target.

Customarily, a target's geometric cross-sectional area, reflectivity, and directivity (the ratio of the power scattered back in the radar's direction to the power that would have been backscattered had the scattering been uniform in all directions—i.e., isotropically) are lumped together in what is called radar cross section (RCS). For computational purposes, this is represented by the Greek letter sigma, and is usually expressed in terms of square meters of area. The power density of the waves reflected back in the radar's direction, then, can be found by multiplying the power density of the transmitted waves when they reach the target by the target's RCS. Since the directivity of a target can be quite high, for some target aspects the RCS may be many times the geometric cross sectional area (the F-15, for instance, has an actual area of approximately 25 sq. meters when viewed from the side; its RCS, however, when viewed from the same aspect, is probably closer to 400 sq. meters; additional aircraft for comparison include the Boeing B-52 with an equivalent RCS of 1,076 sq. ft., the Rockwell B-1A with an RCS of 108 sq. ft., and the Rockwell B-1B, with an RCS of 11 sq. ft.). For others, the reverse may be true.

Regardless, the further away from the radar a target is, the lower the strength of the return echo. Assuming an arbitrary strength of 1 at 1 mile, echoes from a standard target at 50 mile range, for instance, are only 0.00000016 times as strong.

Though work on RAM and lowering RCS continued in many parts of the world during the closing stages of the war, its priority effectively remained low. During 1944, scientists at the prestigious Massachusetts Institute of Technology Radiation Laboratory created a ship-optimized RAM-type product referred to as "Halpern anti-radar paint" (HARP) with iron particulates suspended in a neoprene rubber base, but this saw little use and eventually was discarded. Additionally, and perhaps more importantly, an Air Force-sponsored research project of approximately the same era resulted in the development of a paint referred to as MX-410, which also was a rubber matrix, though differing in having disc-shaped aluminum flakes in place of HARP's iron particulates.

With the post-1950s profligation of radar systems around the world, and an ever-increasing surface-to-air missile barrier rising in what then was considered to be the main U.S. threat—the Soviet Union—interest in RCS and RAM technology began to resurface, though only as a secondary effort behind conventional electronic countermeasures and only at the most highly classified levels of government. In fact, the first aircraft created from scratch with RCS and RAM as integral elements of its design, Lockheed's A-12 high-speed, high-altitude reconnaissance aircraft, was a product of a Central Intelligence Agency requirement rather than that of any of the three major military services.

Work on the A-12 had been initiated during 1959, taking into consideration for the first time

Jay Miller/Aerofax, Inc.

F-117A, 80-0790, begins gear retraction sequence for go-around. All three landing gear retract forward into respective wells. During pass, aircraft sounded like virtually any other jet, though somewhat muted.

Jay Miller/Aerofax, Inc.

Landing roll-out for F-117A, 84-0828. Drag chute was released for ground crew pick-up moments later. Open drag chute compartment doors are visible just ahead of vertical tail surfaces. Visible are still-extended antennas.

the fact that resonance effects on straight portions of reflecting skin materials greater than a half-wavelength in dimension will radiate perpendicularly to the surface when illuminated by radar. It was discovered, however, that if the same surface was curved, the resonance effect would decrease by a mathematically computable ratio and the reflected energy would be distributed in several different directions. Thus curved surfaces returned considerably less energy to a radar receiver than flat.

With this in mind, Lockheed embarked on what was, to all intents and purposes, the first successful RCS-lowering blended fuselage design that combined aerodynamics with the exigencies of diminishing the aircraft's radar return. Chines and wings were successfully blended with the A-12's two engine nacelles and a long, tubular fuselage to create the first Mach 3 cruise-capable aircraft in history. Though 102 ft. long and with a wingspan of 55 ft. 7 in., its total RCS was only 22 sq. in.

Blending of components in the A-12, however, was not the end of Lockheed's initial approach to what became known as "stealth" technology. In addition, the company integrated into the aircraft's basic design RAM-type structural elements called corner reflectors. These devices, which were integral with the wing and fuselage chine leading edge surfaces (thus giving the leading edge surface paneling a saw-tooth or dog-tooth look) were formed from three intersecting, mutually perpendicular metal (titanium) sheets. When installed, they reflected energy like any other metal surface, but the difference was that their triangular configuration created a very effective energy trap. In the A-12, for additional attenuation, a pyroceramic insert matrixed with its own attenuators was used as a filler to give the wing leading edge continuity,

aerodynamic integrity, and the ability to withstand the rigors of cruising flight at three times the speed of sound.

RAM, it was discovered, could be manufactured from a wide variety of materials with each providing a unique or energy-specific capability. Concerning the latter, RAM was found to be most efficient when utilized in thicknesses that were dimensionally a quarter of the specific wavelength being attenuated and also permeable to electromagnetic energy. When applied in layers, energy reflected repeatedly between them was rapidly dissipated and returns were minimized.

Unfortunately, first-generation RAMs came with a hefty price. In many instances, they were applied to external parts of the aircraft and were not load-bearing, and this resulted in both aerodynamic and weight penalties. With the sole exception of the then-highly-classified A-12 (and, it should be mentioned, one of its never-to-be-built competitors, General Dynamics' highly-classified *Kingfish* project; the latter was to have been manufactured almost entirely of pyroceram; it would have been capable of Mach 6.25 at an altitude of 125,000 ft.), they were rarely considered as integral elements of the airframe.

Topping off the attention to lowering the A-12's RCS was a covering of radar absorbent paint (initially this was applied to the most reflective elements, only; later, the entire aircraft was painted). Basically a matrix consisting of a suspension base (epoxy) and ferrite (iron) particulates, it worked on the same fundamental principles of other RAMs in that the molecular structure was optimized to absorb (in the form of "free electron" activity converted to heat) as much of the incoming radar energy as possible. Though only modestly effective (much of the radar's energy was still reflected), when combined with other design

techniques and the more aggressive forms of structural RAM, it provided a rather large payoff in lowering the aircraft's total RCS.

Little information has entered the public domain concerning RAMs and their physical characteristics. The following list, however, was provided by Plessey Microwave of England and gives some insight into this relatively esoteric subject:

A-1 Netting—A broadband, moderate-performance, low-cost material covering 4 GHz up to 94 to 100 GHz. Main applications are reducing RCS outside installations such as hardened aircraft shelter doors. For it to be utilized in harsh environments, it must be encapsulated in a PVC or plastic envelope. It has numerous applications.

Salisbury Screen—If material is needed to work down at a lower than normal operational frequency, it can be utilized in this form, which consists of a back-reflecting mechanism such as a wire mesh, metallic mesh, sheet material, or even a garden fence. There is a dielectric airspace between the absorber on the front surface and the rear surface, with the distance calculated depending on the operating frequency required. At 1 GHz its performance is increased from about 12 or 15 dB to about 20 dB. There is a third harmonic performance from the base frequency (1GHz) at 3 GHz, 5 GHz, 7GHz, and so on.

IRAM—The base material for this is horsehair packing (exactly the same as commonly available for other, more domestic requirements). Its main use is to absorb stray energy and sidelobes from communication antennas. It is inexpensive, but it has moderate performance in the 15 dB range, having a frequency excursion of about 4 GHz up to 16 GHz. It is available in sheets with sizes of 8 ft. by 2 ft.

LA O (La Nought)—A high-performance material consisting of reticulated polyurethane foam treated with carbon emulsions. Its performance (frequency range) is dependent upon the thickness required. At 6mm, it would have a high-performance broadband from approximately 20 GHz up to 100 GHz; in 12mm thickness the bottom frequency would improve with coverage of from 4 GHz to in excess of 50 GHz; in the 2 in. thick version a bottom operating frequency of 1 to 1.5 GHz would be possible, but reasonable performance would occur in the 30 to 50 GHz range. This product has many applications ranging from antennas to missile nosecones. If LA O is "foamed through" with a low-loss dielectric foam, its characteristic is changed into a flexible sheet which is very rigid with a high mechanical strength. In this form, it can be fabricated or molded into virtually any shape desired. Where weight is a significant problem, and flexibility of the product is required, LA O can be machined into whatever is required.

ADRAM (Advanced Dielectric Radar Absorbent Material)—The base material is polyurethane, but it is loaded with a dielectric (plastic or insulating) material. Performance is similar to that of the narrow-band materials. It has a high angle-of-incidence property (it can operate at angles-of-incidence in excess of 120° included angle) whereas the narrow-band materials operate at + or - 50°. The need for high angle-of-incidence performance is to get multi-bounce, multi-path reflections of high-energy, whereas the single-tuned frequencies operate at (basically) 90° to the incoming signal (the original single-frequency materials were used on various aircraft projects during the 1950s, but weight problems precluded widespread use).

Sheet Materials—Using rubbers, nitriles, silicones, and polyurethanes as bases, it is possible to load them with various magnetically-loaded products such as ferrous materials, carbons, and

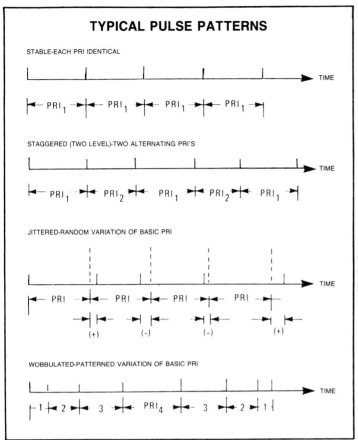

TYPICAL PULSE PATTERNS

STABLE-EACH PRI IDENTICAL

TIME

$\leftarrow$ PRI$_1$ $\rightarrow$ $\leftarrow$ PRI$_1$ $\rightarrow$ $\leftarrow$ PRI$_1$ $\rightarrow$ $\leftarrow$ PRI$_1$ $\rightarrow$

STAGGERED (TWO LEVEL)-TWO ALTERNATING PRI'S

TIME

$\leftarrow$ PRI$_1$ $\rightarrow$ $\leftarrow$ PRI$_2$ $\rightarrow$ $\leftarrow$ PRI$_1$ $\rightarrow$ $\leftarrow$ PRI$_2$ $\rightarrow$ $\leftarrow$ PRI$_1$ $\rightarrow$

JITTERED-RANDOM VARIATION OF BASIC PRI

TIME

$\leftarrow$ PRI $\rightarrow$ $\leftarrow$ PRI $\rightarrow$ $\leftarrow$ PRI $\rightarrow$ $\leftarrow$ PRI $\rightarrow$

(+)   (−)   (−)   (+)

WOBBULATED-PATTERNED VARIATION OF BASIC PRI

TIME

1 2 3 PRI$_4$ 3 2 1

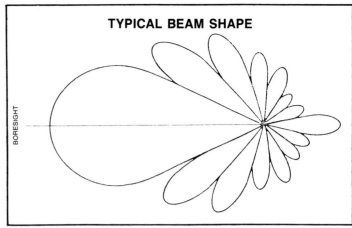

TYPICAL BEAM SHAPE

BORESIGHT

Jay Miller/Aerofax, Inc.

F-117A, 84-0828, was given special "high visibilty" markings for airshow circuit. Aircraft is expected to appear at up to two shows per month during 1989-1990.

high-performance dielectrics. These are high-performance narrow-band items which can be manufactured in mouldings which bond two materials together (for example, one tuned to S-band and one tuned to X-band). The performance is in excess of 25 dB at the chosen operating frequencies. Application is limited because of weight.

Additionally, during the early 1960s, it is known that Lockheed developed and flight tested a first-generation RAM product utilizing a Salisbury Screen and a rubberized coating called Echosorb. This matrix was tested extensively by the company as a U-2 undersurface coating before being shelved due to general ineffectivity and maintenance difficulties. Still more recently, the Japanese company, TDK, revealed that it sells a commercial RAM consisting of two layers of ferrites with different characteristics that can be utilized to absorb microwaves for commercial purposes (such as on tall buildings to absorb television signals or correct problems with television ghosting).

The other passive elements involved in masking an aircraft's presence lie in controlling its infrared (IR) signatures, its accoustical signature, and its exhaust emissions. Infrared radiation is electromagnetic radiation with a dual quality. The principal feature distinguishing IR from radar energy is its position in the electromagnetic spectrum. The frequency of IR radiation extends from approximately one million to five-hundred million megaHertz. In the frequency spectrum, IR falls between the upper limit of microwaves and the lower limit of light. Because of this location, it exhibits some of the characteristics of microwaves and some of the characteristics of light waves. IR, interestingly, can be transmitted through materials opaque to visible light, and IR also can be optically focused by lenses and mirrors. Any material whose temperature is above absolute zero (zero degrees on the Kelvin temperature scale; or -273

degrees centigrade) generates IR radiation. If the material is heated, not only does the kinetic energy of the molecules increase, but also the electrons in each atom are raised to a higher energy level. As the material cools, it gives up this energy and the electrons fall back to their original energy level. This energy level change causes electromagnetic radiations, some of which fall into the IR wavelength range. Because IR is produced by warm materials and because temperature dictates the characteristics of the radiation from these materials, IR energy is often erroneously referred to as "heat waves". IR is not heat, but depends on heat for generation.

The development of IR systems has been paralleled by a search for effective IR countermeasures (IRCM). IRCM can be either specifically designed equipment to affect target homing ability of an IR seeker, or it can be specific tactics designed to affect target discrimination ability. Importantly, through passive elements such as design, the detectability of a target such as an aircraft may be decreased by shielding the hot components of an engine from view or by reducing the engine operating temperature.

Efficient use of some IRCM requires warning of the presence of an IR threat. Since IR systems can attack without the use of a supporting radar search and track system for acquisition, airborne IR warning receivers have been developed to passively detect the presence of the attacker's exhaust plume. Airborne IR warning receivers are capable not only of detecting the presence of an airborne interceptor, but they also can detect the launch of an air-to-air missile. Once the IR homing missile has been launched, IR countermeasures can be employed.

One IR countermeasure is the introduction of smoke into the exhaust of the target aircraft's jet engine(s) to diffuse engine-generated IR radiation.

Another IRCM is the flare. Flares are designed to produce a greater source of IR radiation than

the target aircraft's jet engines. The flare is ejected from the aircraft, and as it falls away, the IR homing missile will track the flare and not the original target aircraft. The major disadvantage of flares is that only a limited number can be carried.

Another IRCM is the use of a powerful IR source, such as a lamp, that can be installed in the tail of an aircraft. By blinking the lamp on and off at a predetermined rate, an IR homing missile can be deceived in much the same way that a radar can be angle-deceived. The advantage of this IRCM type is that the supply of countermeasures does not run out.

Tactical maneuvering is another form of IRCM. The aircraft may be able to evade the IR seeker's field of view, or it may maneuver so as to place the missile's IR detector view into the sun. If the latter maneuver is successful, the missile will not be able to separate the target from background radiation. Maneuvering into a cloud bank where the water droplets and dust particles will absorb and scatter the aircraft IR radiation is another IRCM.

Perhaps the penultimate example of IRCM is represented in the F-117A. Lockheed engineers went to great lengths to ensure that the infrared signature of this aircraft was kept to an absolute minimum. Exhaust gases are mixed with relatively cool ambient air in a plenum just aft of the engine compartment. The cooling air arrives via ducting that brings it from slots located in front of and below the intakes. Once mixed, the exhaust then is passed through a horizontal slot-type nozzle assembly that is some six feet wide and approximately six inches deep. This slot is divided into twelve separate ports which serve to channel the exhaust gases into an extended lower lip which is actually the flattened empennage of the aircraft. There the exhaust gases are again mixed rapidly with ambient air. By the time they enter the aircraft slipstream, temperature levels have been lowered significantly and the exhaust plume presents a minimal infrared target.

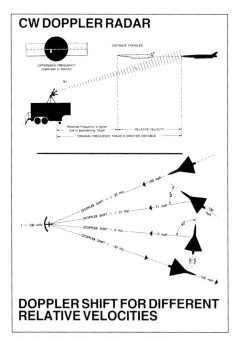

CW DOPPLER RADAR

DOPPLER SHIFT FOR DIFFERENT RELATIVE VELOCITIES

ECHO I AND *HAVE BLUE*:

On August 22, 1980, the following statement by then-Secretary of Defense Harold Brown (under President Jimmy Carter) was released to the public:

"I am announcing today a major technological advance of great military significance.

"This so-called 'stealth' technology enables the United States to build manned and unmanned aircraft that cannot be successfully intercepted with existing air defense systems. We have demonstrated to our satisfaction that the technology works.

"This achievement will be a formidable instrument of peace. It promises to add a unique dimension to our tactical forces and the deterrent strength of our strategic forces. At the same time it will provide us capabilities that are wholly consistent with our pursuit of verifiable arms control agreements, in particular, with the provisions of SALT II.

"For three years, we have successfully maintained the security of this program. This is because of the conscientious efforts of the relatively few people in the Executive Branch and the Legislative Branch who were briefed on the activity and of the contractors working on it.

"However, in the last few months, the circle of people knowledgeable about the program has widened, partly because of the increased size of the effort, and partly because of the debate underway in the Congress on new bomber proposals. Regrettably, there have been several leaks about the stealth program in the last few days in the press and television news coverage.

"In the face of these leaks, I believe that it is not appropriate or credible for us to deny the existence of this program. And it is now important to correct some of the leaked information that misrepresented the Administration's position on a new bomber program. The so-called stealth bomber was not a factor in our decision in 1977 to cancel the B-1; indeed, it was not yet in design.

"I am gratified that, as yet, none of the most sensitive and significant classified information about the characteristics of this program has been disclosed. An important objective of the announcement today is to make clear the kinds of information that we intend scrupulously to protect at the highest security level. Dr. Perry, my Under Secretary of Defense for Research and Engineering and a chief architect of this program will elaborate this point further.

"In sum, we have developed a new technology of extraordinary military significance. We are vigorously applying this technology to develop a number of military aircraft and these programs are showing very great promise.

"We can take tremendous pride in this latest achievement of American technology. It can play a major role in strengthening our strategic and tactical forces without in any way endangering any of our arms control initiatives. And it can contribute to the maintenance of peace by posing a new and significant offset to the Soviet Union's attempt to gain military ascendancy by weight of numbers.

"I would now like to ask Bill Perry to give you some additional details on our stealth program."

Under Secretary of Defense for Research and Engineering William Perry's comments were:

"World War II demonstrated the decisive role that air power can play in military operations. It also demonstrated the potential of radar as a primary means of detecting aircraft and directing fire against them. On balance, though, the advantage clearly was with the aircraft. Subsequent to World War II, defensive missiles—both ground-launched and airlaunched—were developed and "married" with radar fire control systems. This substantially increased the effectiveness of air defense systems, shifting the balance against aircraft. For the last few decades we have been working on techniques to defeat such air defense systems. At present, our military aircraft make substantial use of electronic countermeasures (jamming) and flying low to place themselves in 'ground clutter', both of which degrade the effectiveness of air defense radars. By these means we have maintained the effectiveness of our military aircraft in the face of radar-directed defensive missiles.

"However, the Soviets continue to place very heavy emphasis on the development and deployment of air defense missiles in an attempt to offset the advantage we have in air power. They have built thousands of surface-to-air missile systems, they employ radars with high power and monopulse tracking circuits which are very difficult to jam, and in the last few years they have developed air-to-air missiles guided by 'look down' radars which are capable of tracking aircraft in 'ground clutter'.

"Because of these developments and because of the importance we attach to maintaining our air superiority, we have for years been developing what we call 'penetration' technology—the technology that degrades the effectiveness of radars and other sensors used by air defense systems. A particular emphasis has been on developing that technology which makes an aircraft 'invisible' (a figure of speech) to radar. In the early 1960s, we applied a particular version of this technology to some of our reconnaissance aircraft. In the mid-1970s we applied it to the cruise missiles then being developed (Tomahawk and ALCM). By the summer of 1977 it became clear that this technology could be considerably extended in its effectiveness and could be applied to a wide class of vehicles including manned aircraft. We concluded that it was possible to build aircraft so difficult to detect that they could not be successfully engaged by any existing air defense systems. Recognizing the great significance of such a development we took three related actions: first,

Inverted pole model provides insight into one of the early configuration studies leading up to the final Have Blue *design. Vertical tails were smaller and less swept than those ultimately found on the aircraft as built.*

The first Have Blue *was equipped with a conventional nose boom for airspeed, altitude, angle-of-attack, and sideslip sensing. Primarily an aerodynamic testbed, it served to prove the configuration's flightworthiness.*

Initial ground tests of Have Blue *took place at Lockheed's Burbank, California facility. Engine runs were accomplished outdoors at night after the Burbank airport was closed. Following the runs, the aircraft was partially disassembled and delivered to Groom Lake via Lockheed C-5A on November 16, 1977.*

we made roughly a ten-fold increase in our investment to advance this technology; second, we initiated a number of very high priority programs to apply this technology; and third, we gave the entire program extraordinary security protection, even to the point of classifying the very existence of such a program.

"Initially we were able to limit knowledge of the program to a very few Government officials in both the Executive and Legislative Branches and succeeded in maintaining complete secrecy about the program. However, as the program increased in size—currently the annual funding is 100 times greater than when we decided to accelerate the program in 1977—it became necessary to brief more people. The existence of a stealth program has now become public knowledge. But even as we acknowledge the existence of a stealth program, we will draw a new security line to protect that information about the program which could facilitate a Soviet countermeasures program. We will continue to protect at the highest security level information about:

a. the specific techniques which we employ to reduce detectability;

b. the degree of success of each of these techniques;

c. characteristics of specific vehicles being developed;

d. funds being applied to specific programs; and

e. schedules of specific programs.

"With those ground rules, I think you can see that I am extremely limited in what I can tell you about the program. I will say this. First, stealth technology does not involve a single technical approach, but rather a complex synthesis of many. Even if I were willing to describe it to you, I could not do it. in a sentence or even a paragraph. Second, while we have made remarkable advances in the technology in the last three years, we have been building on excellent work done in our defense technology program over the last two decades. Third, this technology—theoretically at least—could be applied to any military vehicle which can be attacked by radar-directed fire. We are considering all such applications and are moving with some speed to develop those applications which are the most practical and which have the greatest military significance. Fourth, we have achieved excellent success on the program, including flight tests of a number of different vehicles."

As Brown and Perry implied, work on stealth optimized—or low-observable—aircraft had been on-going for a considerable period of time by the date of their 1980 announcement. Many companies, most notably the Lockheed-California operation's Burbank facility and their unique Advanced Development Projects ("Skunk Works") operation (where the U-2, A-12, F-12, SR-71, and D-21 aircraft were developed), had long since forged ahead with reduced radar signature projects of one kind or another, and several, including Lockheed. had resulted in flightworthy hardware.

By late 1975, even though there were then limits to RCS simulation capability, work with the company's Cray computer system had generated a suitable design profile.

During 1974, the Defense Advanced Research Projects Agency (DARPA) requested five major US military aircraft manufacturers to generate preliminary studies calling for a fighter optimized to have significantly reduced radar delectability. As Lockheed had not produced a fighter for nearly ten years, it was not invited to participate.

Consequent to this, the *Skunk Works'* Ben Rich, then deputy to "Kelly" Johnson, asked Johnson to obtain a letter from the CIA granting the *Skunk Works* permission to discuss the SR-71's (and A-12's) low observable characteristics in order to petition for Lockheed to be included in the DARPA project. As a result, the *Skunk Works* was cleared to release information and participate in classified symposia to share the knowledge gained from the A-12 and SR-71 programs. This led to an invitation by DARPA to participate in conceptual studies of low observable techniques, known at the time as *Harvey*.

While Rich and the *Skunk Works'* Ed Martin were maneuvering to get Lockheed approved to participate in *Harvey*, during 1974 and 1975 Lockheed, using internal research and development funds, refined a technique of flight vehicle external shaping that reduced its RCS by several orders of magnitude. This accomplishment was made possible by the development of *Echo 1*, the first practical computer program to very accurately predict the RCS of an air vehicle. Developed by software engineer Denys Overholser and retired Lockheed mathematician Bill Schroeder, it was a major breakthrough...and it gave Lockheed a distinct advantage over any of its competitors.

Schroeder had created *Echo I* by intellectually revisiting a century-old set of mathematical formulas originally derived by Scottish physicist James Clerk Maxwell and refined by turn-of-the-century German electromagnetics expert Arnold Johannes Sommerfeld. These calculations predicted the manner in which a given geometric configuration would scatter (or reflect) electromagnetic radiation.

Russian physicist Pyotr Ufimtsev had taken this early work a step further, developing a more simplified approach that concentrated on electromagnetic currents at the edges of geometric shapes. The Maxwell, Sommerfeld, and Ufimtsev equations were available to anyone...but had been considered too cumbersome to be applied to anything but simple geometric forms.

Lockheed's breakthrough was Schroeder's concept of reducing the complex shape of a traditional aircraft to a finite set of two-dimensional surfaces that could be reasonably analyzed using these calculations. The result was "faceting"—creating a three-dimensional aircraft, not out of smooth, gracefully curved surfaces, but out of a collection of flat panels.

Schroeder realized that by using groups of triangular panels to form a vehicle surface the number of individual radar reflection calculations could be limited to a manageable number. If each flat surface could then be angled in a way that would reflect any incoming radar beam away from its source, and if the combined shape could still create lift, a "stealth" aircraft might be achieveable.

In the rush of competition, Overholser's team was asked to quickly create a revolutionary computer code to solve the problem for the radar crosssection (RCS) of the shape Schroeder envi-

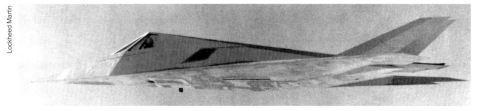

The second Have Blue *was flown a total of 52 times. It joined the flight test program during July of 1978 and differed from the first aircraft in being dedicated to airborne radar cross section testing.*

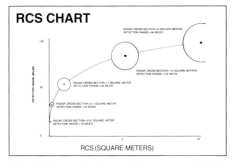

RCS CHART

RADAR CROSS-SECTION = 5 SQUARE METERS
DETECTION RANGE = 84 MILES

RADAR CROSS-SECTION = 10 SQUARE METERS
DETECTION RANGE = 100 MILES

RADAR CROSS-SECTION = 1 SQUARE METER
DETECTION RANGE = 56 MILES

RADAR CROSS-SECTION = 0.1 SQUARE METER
DETECTION RANGE = 32 MILES

RADAR CROSS-SECTION = 0.01 SQUARE METER
DETECTION RANGE = 18 MILES

DETECTION RANGE (MILES)

RCS (SQUARE METERS)

sioned. They arrived at a clever system able to accurately predict the way a faceted aircraft shape would appear on radar. In just five weeks, *Echo I* had been born.

To validate the approach, a simple, idealized aircraft model, nicknamed the *Hopeless Diamond* by its creators, was built and tested at the *Skunk Works* electromagnetics facility in Burbank. Its RCS proved far lower than any shape Lockheed had previously tested. Since range testing of signatures being obtained was beyond the capability of then existing facilities, Lockheed concurrently developed special mounting devices and testing methods to evaluate its new design.

In August of 1975, Lockheed, along with two other contractors (Boeing and Northrop), was invited by DARPA to participate in a competitive effort to develop and test an aircraft known as the Experimental Stealth Testbed (XST) (some sources claim the acronym stood for Experimental Survivable Testbed). In April of 1976 Lockheed was chosen to proceed with detail design, development, and test of this new aircraft. The program was given the name *Have Blue*.

Preliminary design responsibility for the new aircraft at Lockheed was given to Dick Scherer, Warren Gilmour, and Leo Celniker. Program Manager was Norm Nelson and the principle engineers assigned were Ed Baldwin, Alan Brown, Dick Cantrell, Henry Combs, Bob Loschke, the afore-mentioned Denys Overholser, and Bill Taylor. Manufacturing was placed under the direction of Bob Murphy.

Have Blue was a subsonic, single-place aircraft powered by two General Electric J85GE-4A engines. The aircraft was 47 feet 3 inches in length, 7 feet 6-1/4 inches high, and had a wingspan of 22 feet 6 inches with a resultant wing area of 386 sq. feet. The wing planform was a modified delta with a sweep of 72.5°. There were

no flaps, speed brakes, or high lift devices incorporated in the design. The structure was aluminum alloy with steel and titanium utilized in the hot areas. The surface controls were elevons, located inboard on the wing trailing edges, and two all moveable fins at the wing root that were swept back some 35° (leading edge) and canted inboard some 30°. A side stick controller and conventional rudder pedals operated the control surfaces through a fly-by-wire command and stability augmentation system without mechanical back-up. Elevon nose-down pitch control was augmented by a large, two-position flap called the platypus, which was deflected downward automatically whenever 12° angle-of-attack was exceeded.

The aircraft had a tricycle landing gear with main gear antiskid braking. Nose wheel steering was installed on the second aircraft. While the forward retraction insured reliable emergency gear extension, it also meant that takeoff and landing would always occur at the most aft center-of-gravity location.

The test gross weight of the aircraft ranged from approximately 9,200 to 12,500 pounds. Zero fuel weight was 8,950 pounds. Fuel weight was 3,500 pounds and all fuel was carried in fuselage and wing tanks.

The unorthodox *Have Blue* configuration was designed to provide a highly maneuverable fighter aircraft with Verly Low Observable (VLO) characteristics. As a result, the external shape evolved from VLO and controllability characteristics. This resulted in a relaxed static stability (RSS) aircraft which required a quad-redundant, fly-by-wire flight control system (FCS) to provide handling qualities throughout the flight envelope.

The restrictions imposed by VLO requirements were unprecedented and demanded new approaches to preserve efficient propulsion system performance. Each inlet duct was equipped with a flat, RCS treated grid given a porosity sized for the cruise condition. The airflow was augmented at takeoff with blow-in doors mounted on the upper fuselage surface. There was concern that the inlet grids would create problems with engine performance, but these worries proved unfounded. The grids actually had a beneficial side effect in that they helped straighten the vortex disturbed inlet airflow from the highly swept wing leading edges, especially at high angles of attack.

The General Electric J85-GE-4A nonafterburning engines were obtained as Government Furnished Equipment (GFE) from United States

Navy North American T-2B trainer stores. No engine modifications except coating of the spinners was made.

The exhaust system design was likewise driven by VLO requirements. To prevent radar energy from penetrating to the turbine face, the tailpipe was transitioned from a round duct to a 17-to-1 flattened slot convergent nozzle. The trailing edge of each nozzle was terminated on a 54° scarf angle to correspond to the airframe aft closure. Vanes which were interposed and angled in the slot exit helped straighten the exhaust flow back to the longitudinal axis, although some thrust vector "toe-in" remained. Sufficient bypass air was passed over the tailpipe to cool the aft fuselage structure.

The *Have Blue* test program was clearly outlined in the original Development and Demonstration test plan to include: radar cross section and wind tunnel model tests of the prototype design; qualification and proof tests for various systems and subsystems; preflight testing of the assembled aircraft and systems; and finally, flight tests of the aircraft.

As previously stated, the basic configuration was developed utilizing the *Echo I* program. A one-third scale RCS model of the *Have Blue* configuration was tested during December 1975 at the Grey Butte Microwave Measurement facility and a small model in Lockheed Anechoic Chamber. A second series of one-third scale model tests were conducted at Grey Butte in January of 1976. These tests confirmed significant R improvements made with a few minor configration changes.

On the basis of these tests, low and high speed wind tunnel models were fabricated. Only 1,920 hours were required to tailor and define aerodynamic and propulsion characteristics.

A full-scale RCS model was constructed and used at the Air Force Ratscat Backscatter Measurement Range at White Sands, New Mexico to further develop and validate the VLO design. Many detail problems were resolved during this stage, allowing manufacture of th two test aircraft to proceed rapidly.

The initial engine runs were accomplished on the first *Have Blue* aircraft on November 4 1977 at Lockheed's Burbank facility. In order to maintain security, the aircraft was parke between two semi-tractor-trailers over which camouflage net had been installed. The runs were performed at night after the airport was closed. The biggest problem

F-117A pole model under construction at Lockheed's Burbank facility. Built to explore radar cross section attributes, it eventually gave credence to what had previously been only computer generated numbers.

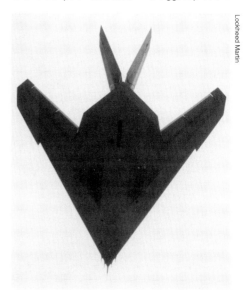

Leading edge extensions were tested on 780 in an attempt to reduce takeoff and landing speeds.

experienced was a phone call from a local resident who wanted to know what was making all the noise. Following the engine runs, the aircraft was partially disassembled (the wings were removed) and readied for shipment. It was delivered to the test location, via C-5A, on November 1, 1977. Since this was the first time a C-5A had operated from the Burbank airport, the morning traffic became substantially more congested as people strained to see this "aluminum overcast" that appeared to hover over the city during its departure.

The aircraft was off-loaded at the Groom Lake and reassembled. Since most of the systems had been checked out in Burbank, only a few System Check Outs (SCOs) needed to be accomplished prior to first flight...which would be conducted under the direction of *Have Blue* Flight Test Manager Dick Miller. Engine thrust runs were performed and a series of four low and high speed taxi tests were conducted. During the third taxi test a problem developed that would become a nuisance throughout the program. In particular, overheated brakes which caused the wheel fuse plugs to melt. Flight control system performance was carefully monitored during the taxi tests and some minor changes were made to the yaw gains. Successful drag chute operation was verified and, following the fourth taxi test, the aircraft was deemed ready to fly.

On December 1, 1977, with Lockheed test pilot Bill Park at the controls, *Have Blue* lifted into the air. A new era in military aviation had just begun. Only twenty months had passed since contract award,

As previously noted, the primary objective of the test program was to demonstrate VLO technology. Towards this end, *Have Blue* 1001 would demonstrated loads/flutter, performance handling qualities, and stability and control. *Have Blue* 1002 was designated as the RCS test vehicle.

Have Blue 1001 accomplished 36 flights over the next 5 months and successfully expanded the flight envelope sufficiently to allow the RCS testing to be performed. Unfortunately, on May 4, 1978, the aircraft sustained major damage during an attempted landing at less than design landing speed and had to be abandoned in flight by Park.

Have Blue 1002 joined the program during July 1978 and flew for the first time on July 20 with Air Force pilot Norman "Ken" Dyson at the controls. This aircraft differed from *Have Blue* 1001 in that it possessed a "real" airspeed system (no nose boom) and did not have a drag chute installed. It also incorporated nose wheel steering to improve ground handling, and was adorned with all the coatings and materials required to perform its intended task. Following some airspeed calibration flights, the aircraft accomplished 52 flights during the following 12 months and completed the low observable testing.

Have Blue's pitot static system consisted of three separate static sources on the upper and lower forebody surfaces and three total pressure probes; one at the nose tip and two on the windshield center post. *Have Blue* 1001 also had a flight test nose boom which included pitot-static pressure sources and angle-of-attack and sideslip vanes. A flight path accelerometer (FPA) also was included as part of the basic airspeed probe and was located inside the probe at the angle-of-attack vane position. The forebody static pressure position error, determined from flight tests, agreed very well with wind tunnel data. The gear down position error, however, was less than the wind tunnel results. It should be noted that the design concepts of this airplane severely limited the choices of static and total pressure locations and,

F-117A production inside Plant B-6 at Burbank. These aircraft would become the last Skunk Works aircraft manufactured at the old Burbank site as all new production would afterwards take place at Palmdale.

as a result, the static pressure position errors were quite large but were consistent.

Engine out characteristics were unusual in that rolling and yawing moments were in the direction of the operative engine, and more control effort was required in the roll axis than the yaw axis.

Baseline inflight RCS testing was completed during September of 1978. After several modifications required by the results of the baseline testing were completed, penetration testing against ground based radars and IR systems was begun. IR detections matched predictions well. When a T-38 participated in or duplicated the test profiles, it was tracked to the maximum range of the terminal.

The final phase of testing in a simulated integrated air defense environment was completed during July of 1979. The aircraft demonstrated its VLO capabilities against ground and airborne systems during these tests. Its low acoustic signature was also verified. Measured RCS data correlated well with those measured at Ratscat. Unfortunately, *Have Blue* 1002 also was lost when it was written-off at Groom Lake on July 11, 1979 after having completed 52 flights.

The project management of the *Have Blue* program for both the government and Lockheed can be characterized as small, close knit, streamlined, and tailored to the specific needs of the program objectives.

The project was accomplished with daily verbal and secure electronic communications between Lockheed and government program managers supplemented by frequent visits and more formal program reviews. Technical, schedule and cost performance tracking and reporting, although in simplified form, was accurate, timely, and responsive to customer needs.

Evidence of good contingency planning activity on *Have Blue* included actions taken to recover from: the non-availability of significant GFAE items, workarounds and rapid recovery from a three month IAM strike, and reactivation of flight test operations at Groom Lake.

Contractor interfaces were limited, but very important and well managed on the *Have Blue* program. General Electric was a subcontractor for J85 engine installation and performance interface. Lear Siegler was the principle

subcontractor responsible for manufacture and field support of the flight control system.

Lockheed's security program was also quite successful during the *Have Blue* program. It initially started as a "white world" program with minimum security classification requirements. This security posture remained until early 1977 when the government realized that a major breakthrough had been achieved in VLO technology, with great potential to national defense. Subsequently, the program was placed under the "special access required" (SAR) security umbrella. From that point forward Lockheed maintained total secrecy of the program.

Have Blue was made possible by a great deal of contractor/customer cooperation in successfully achieving technical breakthroughs. The ability to reduce high risk technical areas on an accelerated basis and in a cost effective manner was demonstrated by the fact that design, manufacture, and test of this innovative aircraft was accomplished in three years. The VLO aircraft, including engine inlets and exhausts, featured faceted surfaces covered with RAM. Adequate stability and control of the basically unstable aircraft was provided by a quad-redundant fly-by-wire flight control system, with unique *Have Blue* features and some basic components adapted from the F-16 system. The radical design involved breakthroughs in virtually all aircraft design disciplines.

Areas of improvement for follow-on programs were defined by the flight test results. In particular: door closure designs were modified during the flight test program to provide more positive closing forces; fin and rudder installations were improved by relocating at the centerline instead of outboard (heat input was then reduced and potential gaps were eliminated); air data probes were placed further forward to reduce air data correction factors; the handling quality requirements in Mil-F-8785B were inadequate for the design of the FCS required for the *Have Blue* aircraft (*Have Blue's* fixed side stick control was not totally satisfactory for many piloting tasks; lack of stick motion, stick orientation relative to seat location, and the need for lateral constraints for the pilots were all identified as areas requiring improvement); the large flat plate upper surface of the platypus was unevenly heated when engine power settings were changed and the resulting differential expansion caused distortions which warped the surface (this

Four of the F-117A's Combined Test Force five aircraft fleet--Nos. 781, 782, 783, and 831--are seen in formation during a March, 1991 test flight. By the date of this photograph, No. 780, the first Full-Scale Development (FSD) F-117A, had been retired from active flight duty.

distortion combined with manufacturing tolerances associated with the nozzles to make the thrust vector toe-in angles asymmetric; the side forces generated by the asymmetry were picked up by the lateral accelerometer used in the FCS for directional stability augmentation; the resulting commands to the fins caused the aircraft to fly "crabbed", thus requiring the pilot to retrim the aircraft directionally each time that the flight condition changed; the automatic yaw trim feature in the FCS was a partial solution, but the final solution involved elimination of the lateral accelerometer and substitution of a direct measurement of the side slip angle for directional stability augmentation; and the aerodynamic stability and control parameters derived from flight test results with the modified maximum likelihood estimator (MMLE) technique were in good agreement with wind tunnel predictions except for directional stability which was lower than predicted (aircraft with unorthodox nozzle configuraitons and low inherent directional stability require special wind tunnel testing techniques, including flowing nozzles and inlets).

The *Have Blue* program was a low cost demonstration of a radically new concept in VLO aircraft design. *Have Blue* program accomplishments included from a technical standpoint: lowest RCS aircraft in the world by several orders of magnitude; VLO infrared signature; VLO visual signatures; VLO acoustic signature; and confirmation of complex aerodynamics. From a schedule standpoint: 20 months from prototype contract award to first flight; and 88 test sorties. From a cost standpoint; $43 million total; $32.6 million Air Force/DARPA funding; and $10.4 million from Lockheed. In conclusion, it was determined VLO tactical and strategic aircraft could be designed, produced, and operated.

F-117 DEVELOPMENT AND FLIGHT TEST:

During 1978, following an assessment of the prototype results, the Air Force moved ahead with a decision to develop a full-scale production version of the original Lockheed design under the program codename *Senior Trend*. By now, mission objectives had been generated and it thus had become possible for Lockheed to narrow its design focus. The attributes of the aircraft's low RCS were ideally suited for ground support missions, and as a result the production aircraft was designed around that very specific requirement.

The new aircraft was to be optimized to covertly penetrate dense threat environments and attack high value targets with pinpoint weapon accuracy. Heavy emphasis would be placed on making the aircraft totally autonomous, totally passive, and as elusive a target as technologically possible; it would not be dependent upon external communications of any kind in order to accomplish its mission. Heavy emphasis would be placed on maintaining an almost negligible RCS, lowering the infrared (IR) signature, reducing the noise (acoustical) signature, reducing visibility (via size and paint constraints), and reducing powerplant visible emissions (exhaust particulates and contrail generation).

The advantages of very low observables or stealth technology, once successfully demonstrated by Lockheed's *Have Blue* prototypes, quickly led to a full-scale engineering development contract award from the Air Force on November 16, 1978. The fixed price production contract was signed thirteen months later. It called for five full-scale development (FSD) and fifteen production models of a single-seat, subsonic attack aircraft to be officially designated F-117A. Under Program Manager Norm Nelson (working under the direction of the *Skunk Works'* Vice President and General Manager, Ben Rich), engineering on the new aircraft proceeded at a rapid pace, utilizing the data base that had been developed under *Have Blue*. Principle engineers assigned to the new aircraft were Ed Baldwin, Alan Brown, Dick Cantrell, Bob Loschke, and Bill Taylor...all veterans of the earlier low-observables program. Bob Murphy again was tapped to direct manufacturing.

The resulting unusual shape of the F-117A is the end product of the low-observables goals set for the aircraft at the program's beginning. Not surprisingly, it provided the aerodynamic and stability and control engineers with a significant challenge. A major effort was instituted to minimize performance penalties and provide satisfactory flight characteristics. In the end, these efforts were quite successful.

The F-117A incorporates a variety of design features to significantly reduce aircraft signature. There are seven different types of observable signatures of concern: radar, infrared, visual, contrails, engine smoke, acoustics, and electromagnetic emissions. The three signature characteristics providing the greatest potential for exploitation by threat systems are radar, infrared and electromagnetic emissions. The F-117A was designed to minimize these signatures. Techniques utilized include highly swept surfaces, radar absorbing structure and materials, gridded inlets, highaspect-ratio two-dimensional exhaust nozzles, internal weapons carriage, special antennas, and radio frequency transmission techniques.

Since the F-117A was a departure from normal aerodynamic design, a significant effort was made to reduce development risk by using several proven systems from existing aircraft. Examples include: the General Electric F404 turbofan engine used in the McDonnell Douglas F/A-18 fighter; cockpit components from the General Dynamics (now Lockheed Martin) F-16 and the McDonnell Douglas F/A-18; navigation and attack systems; computer and electronics; offthe-shelf weapons; and a modified fly-by-wire F-16 flight control system.

All aircraft designs are a compromise in one form or another, with the primary mission objective dominating these characteristics. The primary mission of the F-117A is to penetrate enemy airspace, destroy high value targets and survive. As a result, low observability became the dominant design factor. Instead of an aerodynamic shape optimized for high speed orlong range, the shape was faceted for purposes of lowering the radar cross section.

Once Dick Cantrell, the *Skunk Works'* chief aerodynamicist, recovered from the initial shock that Alan Brown, the *Skunk Works'* low observables expert, had given him, he set out to achieve the desired compromises and still have a flyable aircraft. This proved a sizable challenge .

Since low observability—or stealth—was the primary goal, it established the external configuration and in particular the sweep angles of the

A modestly large family of weapons, including the GBU-10 (laser guided bomb) have been cleared for use with the F-117A and several others have been specifically developed for Nighthawk *missions.*

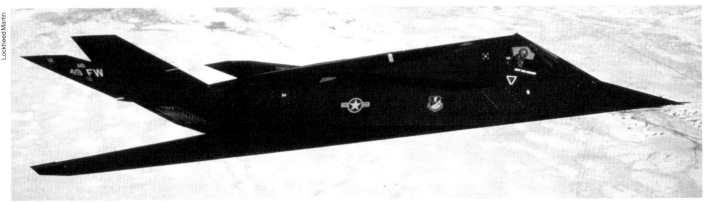

The F-117A is now assigned to the 49th Fighter Wing based at Holloman AFB, New Mexico. Three squadrons are assigned to the 49th, these being the 7th, 8th, and 9th. Several operational aircraft have been lost to accidents over the past few years, but no replacements have been built to maintain inventory levels.

wings and tail. One of the larger challenges was to provide as much sweep as possible and still have sufficient aspect ratio for the needed lift-over-drag (L/D) to achieve the required range. This was accomplished by carrying the wing as far aft as possible in order to increase the span. The trailing edge of the delta was notched-out both for low observables considerations as well as to reduce wetted area.

Another major challenge was to provide adequate control to achieve the desired maneuverability within a reasonable angle-of-attack range for an unstable aircraft in both pitch and yaw. Since horizontal tails were not to be used, large full-span elevons were provided for both pitch and roll control. These were sized to handle the pitch instability which resulted in more roll control power than was needed.

The highly-swept V-tail surfaces were another concession to low observability. The objective was to reduce the height and size yet still provide adequate control for the unstable yaw axis. This required all-movable surfaces.

Alternate means of directional control were investigated, such as split elevon tips, but the V-tail was preferred to provide adequate control power and reduce drag.

The resulting control configuration was not conducive to low takeoff and landing speeds. The full-span elevons could not be drooped for landing without leading edge devices or another means of pitch control. The solution was to use a drag chute for landing and accept a longer takeoff roll. The brake system capacity was subsequently improved reducing reliance on the drag chute.

Another low observability design consideration was to provide very sharp leading edges. This is good for a supersonic airfoil, but not optimum for a subsonic aircraft.

Since this was the first aircraft designed by electrical engineers, it was not surprising that a number of aerodynamic "sins" were committed. In fact, when unaugmented, the F-117A exhibits just about every mode of unstable behavior possible—longitudinal and directional instability, pitch-up, pitch-down, dihedral reversal, and various other cross-axis couplings. Because of these characteristics, there was no question about what kind of flight control system was required. Piloted simulation showed it had to be a full-time, fly-by-wire command augmentation system. Any mechanical back-up flight control system would just add weight since pilot control was impossible without stability augmentation.

When the F-117A program started, the F16 was just being introduced into squadron service and the F/A-18 was just beginning flight test. Since there was already enough risk in the new Skunk Works program, it proved prudent to use developed, off-the-shelf components to the maximum

extent possible not only to reduce risk but also to reduce costs even if it meant some weight penalty. It was decided that the technology developed for the F-16 flyby-wire flight control system was the only one mature enough to be low risk and also relatively low cost due to the volume of production. The F-16 actuators, the flight control computer chassis, and power supplies were modified slightly to adapt them to the F-117A. New control laws had to be developed for implementation in the flight control computer, new interfaces for the new air data sensors defined, and a different actuator failure detection and redundancy management scheme developed. The air data probes and pilot's control stick were developed especially for the F-117A.

The pitch axis was implemented as a g-command system optimized for flight path control to support the ground attack mission. An angle-of-attack (AoA) limiter was incorporated to prevent departures and the elevons were sized to provide the necessary pitch control power. Because the pitch axis control required large elevons, the available roll control power was much more than needed and the flight control computer incorporated authority limiters to keep the roll rate down to minimize structural loads. The four elevons are used for roll control, and roll rate feedback is used to improve the roll damping.

The directional axis control is of particular interest since the F-117A is directionally unstable over large parts of its operational envelope. Operating the weapon bay doors makes it more unstable so that two large all-moveable fins were required to provide the necessary control power. Because of its shape, the aircraft has very low side force...which means that use of a conventional lateral accelerometer feedback for directional stability augmentation was not practical. The air data probes measure differential pressure and the flight control computer acting through the fins literally keeps the nose aligned with the relative wind. Yaw rate and roll rate are fed back to give the desired levels of dutch roll damping and the product of pitch rate and roll rate is fed back to cancel

inertia coupling. The directional axis also incorporates an automatic yaw trim when the gear is up and the pilot is not using the rudder pedals. This feature greatly simplified emergency procedures following an engine failure at lift-off since the pilot only has to retract the gear and concentrate on maintaining AoA and bank angle at the desired values.

Series trim is implemented in all three axes; that is, the stick and pedals are at neutral when the aircraft is in trim. Also, the stick does not move when the autopilot is operating. The autopilot incorporates pitch and roll attitude hold and heading hold with control stick steering (CSS). The CSS disables the autopilot while the pilot maneuvers to a new attitude or heading with the stick and then holds the new attitude when the stick is released. The autopilot also incorporates altitude hold, Mach hold, and automatic navigation.

The net result of the F-117A's flight control system development is an aircraft with comparable pitch and roll response to that of conventionally shaped contemporary fighter and attack aircraft within certain boundaries. It is very maneuverable and fully aerobatic.

The F-117A flight test program began with a series of flights in the Calspan NT-33A where the suitability of the flight control laws was checked and where the effects of some aerodynamic variations were investigated. One of the variations assumed that the directional stability was even worse than predicted so that the pilot could see the effects and get some experience.

The actual first flight of the F-117A, under the direction of program Flight Test Manager Dick Abrams, took place in broad daylight (for safety reasons) on June 18, 1981 with Skunk Works test pilot Harold "Hal" Farley, Jr. at the controls. Since the air data probes were of a new design and had exhibited some pitch yaw coupling during vibration testing, it was decided to ballast the aircraft to a forward center of gravity location and turn off the AoA and beta measurements to the FLCC to prevent any possible coupling. Switches were incorporated in the cockpit for the pilot to activate the

F-117A, No. 826, taxies in following landing at Holloman AFB, New Mexico. Open drag chute compartment, tail code, and other contemporary markings are readily visible.

CONVENTIONAL RADAR COUNTERING TECHNIQUES

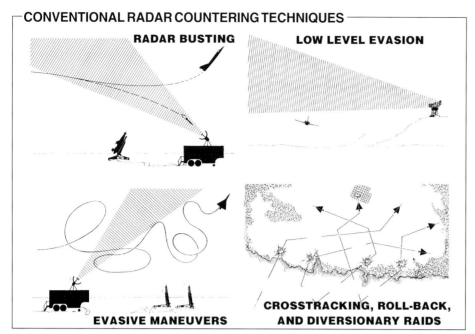

RADAR BUSTING

LOW LEVEL EVASION

EVASIVE MANEUVERS

CROSSTRACKING, ROLL-BACK, AND DIVERSIONARY RAIDS

AIR-TO-AIR MISSILE GUIDANCE SYSTEMS

AI IN TARGET TRACKING MODE

1. COMMAND GUIDANCE
   AI Maintains Radar Track of Both Target and Missile Coded Signals Guide Missile to Target

3. SEMI-ACTIVE RADAR HOMING
   AI Maintains Radar Track, Missile Receives Radar Echo for Guidance to Target

3. SEMI-ACTIVE RADAR HOMING
   AI Maintains Radar Track; Missile Receives Radar Echo for Guidance to Target

4. INFRARED HOMING
   Missile Maintains Track from IR Energy Emitted by Target

AoA and beta feedbacks after attaining a stabilized flight condition at 15,000 feet. Extenders were installed on those switches so they could quickly be turned on if needed.

Immediately after lift off, it became apparent that the directional stability was significantly worse than predicted and the beta feedback to the flight control computer was immediately switched on. Fortunately, the probes worked exactly as predicted, the aircraft stiffened up directionally, and

the rest of the flight was more or less routine. This experience once again showed the value of using in-flight simulation to investigate possible aerodynamic variations prior to first flights. As it turned out, both the directional stability and directional control power were less than predicted and the fins were increased in size by 50% to get back up to the original predicted levels of stability and control power.

Stealthy air data sensors were a unique design challenge. Ideally, flush-mounted "invisible" sensors such as pressure ports on the forebody could be used. Unfortunately, *Skunk Works* engineers could not find four independent locations for AoA and beta (actually sixteen places on the aircraft) without all variables being functions of all others (AoA, beta, Mach, and q) which would require too many correction coefficients in the flight control system. As a result, four probes (for quadruple redundancy) are utilized.

These probes were made of special materials in an unconventional shape which required a lot of test flying to get good position error calibrations on AoA, beta, airspeed, and altitude. Initial designs cracked when the heat was turned on, calibrations shifted, and quality control problems

in probe manufacture required testing and retesting until deficiencies were identified and eliminated.

High angle-of-attack flight test to verify the adequacy of the AoA limiter was approached with extreme caution and took a lot of test time to complete. There were two reasons for this. The first was that all the wind tunnel tests showed that pitch-up would occur at high AoA. Free flight testing of unpowered models verified that pitch-up and deep stall were possible, but that there were no identifiable spin modes. The second reason was that the high AoA tests were done without a recovery chute. There was never any intention to deliberately depart the aircraft because the small model free flight tests showed that all departures eventually wound up in a deep stall. Since there was a possibility that the normal drag chute would effect a recovery from that condition, it was decided that the high AoA testing could go forward without the installation of a special recovery chute.

Flutter testing became a bigger effort than originally planned as a result of a chain of events that started with the aircraft's original design. The big surprise came when an Air Force test pilot was flying a stores compatibility test mission. While performing a sideslip maneuver, explosive flutter of the left fin occurred. The fin was almost completely lost and the pilot brought the F-117A home with difficulty...and with considerably less directional stability than before. As noted earlier, the original fin was 50% smaller than the final version due to directional stability considerations. The corrective action was to increase the fin area by extending the fin edges, but without changing the size of the fin box structure. The net result was a reduction of fin stiffness.

Prior to this incident, an extensive flight flutter clearance program had been conducted, the results of which indicated there were no aeroelastic problems of any significance. Analysis performed subsequent to the incident revealed the problem to be a flutter mode, known as the "hump" mode, that was considered at first to have a flat damping trend that was actually found to be potentially flutter critical. In fact, the aircraft had been cleared to and flown many times at the incident flight conditions before the fin flutter problem was encountered.

The subsequent investigation also revealed that this critical mode, along with others, was highly affected by rudder post bearing friction, which had masked the criticality of the mode in earlier flutter testing. In order to test the absolute worst case (no friction) low friction roller bearings were installed in the test aircraft replacing (for test purposes only) the standard journal bearings on

TYPICAL AAA BATTERY LAYOUT

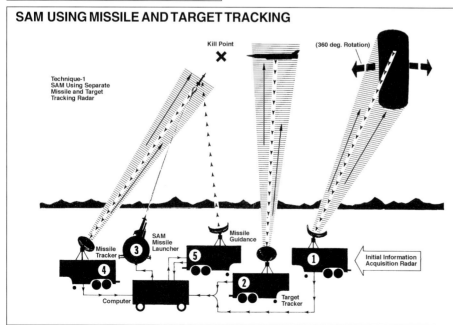

Tracking Radar

Computer

Acquisitio Radar

SAM USING MISSILE AND TARGET TRACKING

Kill Point

(360 deg. Rotation)

Technique-1
SAM Using Separate Missile and Target Tracking Radar

Missile Tracker

3

SAM Missile Launcher

5

Missile Guidance

1

Initial Information Acquisition Radar

4

Computer

2

Target Tracker

the rudder posts. The testing continued and verified satisfactory stability levels of the fin modes out to the desired speeds.

However, the flutter test results did show a significant loss of damping in sideslips. This loss, when coupled with the masking effect of the bearing friction, led to the fin flutter incident. Since then, the fins have been replaced with new fins made of graphite-thermoplastics. These new fins are much stiffer and have demonstrated a very large flutter margin.

The requirements for structural flight tests were fairly typical of a normal aircraft. All of the standard maneuvers had to be performed out to the structural limits of the aircraft. Two problems arose. The first was due to a change in fuel transfer sequencing which reduced the inertia relief provided by wing fuel. This stopped flight testing until a strengthening of the aft wing attach points was accomplished. The second problem occurred when the aft fuselage loads measured in flight test turned out to be significantly higher than predicted by analysis. After much speculation without a reasonable explanation, it was decided to install pressure taps on the rear of the aircraft and compare the pressure distribution results from flight test with those from the wind tunnel. The tunnel data matched the flight test results. This led the *Skunk Works* engineers to look for other sources of loading...which turned out to be the effect of the unusual exhaust system. Trying to take the thrust and squeeze it out of a highaspect-ratio two-dimensional nozzle resulted in some unusual down bending moments which had not been accounted for in the analysis.

Engine tests also were conducted due to the unorthodox design of the exhaust nozzles. Problems were known to occur when a circular thrust pattern is expelled from a round engine then turned and flattened to exhaust out of a long, flat, two-dimensional nozzle. Hot spots, loads, tailpipe distortion, etc. had to be overcome requiring many tests and engineering exercises before a suitable exhaust configura- tion was developed.

One other area of concern also was the distortion produced by the inlet grids and the engines' ability to tolerate this. Analysis indicated the grids should be no problem, but a little skepticism remained. The distortion levels in fact proved to be less than expected and the grids actually acted as flow straighteners giving a consistent source of air to the engine throughout the entire AoA and beta range of the aircraft.

A great deal of icing tunnel work was conducted as a result of inlet icing concerns. This indicated that the inlet grids not only looked like a giant ice cube tray, but acted like one, as well. Later, inflight icing tests using the normal buildup approach were undertaken. It was concluded that a special de-icing system would have to be devised. As a result, the aircraft was equipped with a special wiper system complete with alcohol dispensing capability.

With the F-117A's handling qualities so dependent on good air data, the criticality of pitot-static probe deicing was obvious. Requirements forced upon the aircraft by the low-observables engineering group made the design of the probes and their deicing system a serious challenge. Many different designs were tunnel tested before an acceptable one was found. Airborne results proved the systems worked well. The only real modification required was the repositioning of the icing detector within the engine inlet.

The development of the F-117A avionics systems continues to be an ever-evolving program of changes, upgrades, and improvements. Early FSD testing brought the initial avionics architecture to an initial operational capability during October of 1983. Full capability development after initial operational capability brought most avionics systems to maturity. The Weapon System Computer Subsystem (WSCS) upgrade brought needed computational capability improvements to the F-117A while the Offensive Combat Improvement Program (OCIP) brought additional pilot situational awareness and reduced workload to the night single-seat attack mission. Ongoing programs and planned future capabilities will continue the evolutionary process.

The F-117A avionics systems development followed the same principles as the main airframe program: minimize development risks by using off-the-shelf hardware where possible, modify existing equipment where feasible, and invent new systems only when absolutely required. In this regard, the program was highly successful; however, some of the off-the-shelf and modified systems provided inadequate performance until additiona l improvements were made.

The stealth requirement for avionics design was just as stringent as the basic airframe and required substantial integration of the airframe/avionics systems. Avionics system designs must be aware that electromagnetic emissions from the aircraft, such as radar, are just as vulnerable to detectability as any of the other observables.

Considerable effort went into the incorporation of features to preclude any emission from the F-117A. In the aircraft's stealthy mode, the F-117A is incapable of any emission which may cause detection; i.e., UHF, IFF, radar altimeter, TACAN, etc. The laser target designator is the only exception and considerable forethought went into the amount of time and conditions under which it may fire. As a result, the avionics design of the F-117A operates independently of any

F-117A, 806, during open house at Offutt AFB, Nebraska on September 4, 1995. Aircraft bears "Flying Knights" logo painted horizontally on vertical tail tips.

The F-117A's flat-plate surfaces result in an extraordinarily unorthodox aerodynamic configuration. Flyi-by-wire with computer interfacing is mandatory for aircraft control.

The F-117A embodies virtually all contemporary combat aircraft disciplines. Optimized to meet various low-observables criteria, it is a bizarre, yet practical design.

13

F-117A of the 422nd TES (code WA). All navigation lights, the rotating beacon, and related items are removed when the aircraft is actually used in combat.

active emission and relies completely on passive systems for navigation, target acquisition, and weapon delivery.

As a result of the need to minimize development risks and maximize the use of off-the-shelf equipment, the cockpit became a mix of then state-of-the-art glass cockpit technology and Century series aircraft type switches, lights, and dials. Much of the equipment came from front line aircraft, such as the F/A-18, but the aircraft includes components from practically every aircraft built since the T-33. Examples include parts taken from the SR-71, the P-3, the C-130, the L-1011, the S-3, the F-104, the P-2, and many others.

The main cockpit layout is the now familiar arrangement of Multifunction Displays with a HUD and center sensor display. During F117A conceptual design, the F/A-18 was the only US fighter using a similar arrangement. Due to limitations within the computer system and for risk reduction, most of the warning lights, indicators, and aircraft systems switches are external to the avionics architecture and have no provisions for control from the displays.

Most of the cockpit systems are derived from the F/A-18. These include the early multifunction display indicators, the HUD, fuel gauge, engine instruments, stick grip, and throttles. The sensor display is provided by Texas Instruments and is derived from the Vietnam-era OV-1 OD and P-3C programs.

The original avionics architecture was a dis-tributed real-time processing system which used three Delco M362F computers from the F16 interconnected with a dual redundant MILSTD-1553 data bus. The computers interface with the displays, controls, INS, autopilot, stores management system (SMS), and the sensor systems. The weapon delivery computer (WDC) was the system executive. Beside providing over-all control, the WDC serviced and updated the cockpit displays, performed the weapon delivery ballistics calculations, interfaced to the various sensor systems, and controlled the data distribution. The navigation control computer performed all navigation and control functions including the inertial measurement unit, the control display unit, navigation steering, flight director steering, position update, attitude heading reference system integration, and the TACAN and ILS interface. The third computer provided control and data processing for an additional sensor system and was used as a back-up computer if one of the other two should fail. A data transfer module interface unit was provided to load preflight mission data via a data transfer module from the mission data planning system.

The underlying operating principle of the avionics system is the cueing of the sensor to the target via a precision navigation system thus providing updated target information for accurate weapons release.

Given suitably accurate information about the location of a target and given the excellent accuracy of the onboard inertial system, the computer system cues the infrared (IR) system to the target. The field of view of the IR system being small, requires not only that the position accuracy of the INS be very good but also that the target location data be very accurate so that the IR system can be pointed very accurately. This was the critical program issue for the avionics system. Would sufficiently good target information be available and would system performance be good enough to be able to find a target at night looking only through a small IR window? And, of course, could weapons be delivered accurately enough to destroy the target? Given that the desired target is within the field of view of the IR system, i.e., the pilot can see it on the sensor display, the pilot refines the aiming, designates the target, and consents for weapon release, which occurs via the SMS at the appropriate time.

The infrared acquisition and detection system (IRADS) was built by Texas Instruments. This was an off-the-shelf single turret system that was adapted to a twin turret design due to the unique "in contour" mounting requirements of the F-117A. Stealth characteristics of the F-117A required that the unique exterior shape be maintained. Since there was a need to be able to see from just above the horizon to well behind the aircraft, a forward-looking IR (FLIR) turret and a downward-looking IR (DLIR) were required. This need doubled the size of the servo controller unit and the video tracker unit. Due to the mounting arrangement in the aircraft, the DLIR is inverted relative to the FLIR and thus required the video to be inverted electronically when displayed to the pilot. This led to some interesting calibration and alignment problems. But, any turret may still be mounted in either position.

The F-117A employs screens over the FLIR and DLIR cavities to maintain its low observable signature. The original screens were to be etched metal units from a process not unlike printed circuit boards. These screens proved unable to take the acousti environment of the cavities, in particular the DLIR cavity where the screen broke on its first flight. This breakage led to a vibration and acoustics investigation of the cavities and redesign of the screens. Both FLIR and DLIF cavities now feature acoustic shrouds to limit acoustic affects. The screens are redesigned woven wire units capable of handling the acoustic loads.

The weapon bays are each equipped with a trapeze for loading and raising the weapons. Early concerns for possible damage to the aircraft and bay doors from fin scheduled weapons, like the GBU-10, required that these weapons be dropped trapeze down. This was a major detectability problem for the aircraft. Early weapon certification was performed in this configuration. Later efforts by the aerodynamics department indicated that adequate clearance could be maintained with the trapeze up. This reduced the exposure times by more than a factor of 5. However, some weapons did end up with small speed restrictions due to weapon bay dynamics or airflow disturbances in the near flow field.

The Delco M362F computers were long known to be just adequate for the computational tasks of the F-117A. At the time of their selection, the MIL-STD-1750A instruction set computers that were on the horizon were still too big a risk. The first several years of software development prior to first flight were just as involved with getting the OFP to fit and run in the computer as much as with implementing capabilities.

During 1984, the weapon system computational subsystem (WSCS) upgrade program was started to replace the Delco M362F computers. The IBM Federal Systems AP-102 MILSTD-1750A computer was selected. This was a repack-

All three landing gear assemblies retract forward. All gear wells are equipped with special doors with prism-like edges that are optimized to reduce radar return. Visible in this view are the closed weapon bay doors.

aged version of the same computer used in the Rockwell International *Space Shuttle.*

The architecture for the WSCS computer upgrade was similar to the WDC version with some improvements. Three AP-102 computers were used with each computer controlling a dual redundant MIL-STD-1553 bus for a total of three in the system. The onboard systems were divided between buses 1 and 2 with the third computer and bus held as spares for growth. A unique high speed bus was incorporated for direct communications between the three AP-102s and the expanded data transfer module interface unit.

The aircraft was also enhanced by the decision to expand the weapon release capability from the use of a single weapon bay per pass to the ability to use both weapon bays. This was a significant change as the weapon bay doors, actuators, hydraulics, SMP, and cockpit controls all required redesign and modification .

With the growth potential of the WSCS computers, the program was positioned to embark upon introducing a number of new capabilities. Among the first of these was the incorporation of a significant new weapon capability. The GBU-27 laser guided bomb (LGB) brought new levels of accuracy and target penetration to the guided weapon inventory.

The GBU-27 was the marriage of a modified GBU-24 low-level laser guided bomb seeker, sometimes known as *Paveway 3,* and the BLU-109 improved 2,000 pound warhead. Changes to the GBU-24 seeker included modified canards to fit inside the F-117A weapon bays and a firmware change for trajectory shaplng .

The GBU-27 features two guidance modes, each optimized to achieve the best penetration angle for horizontally or vertically oriented targets. The trajectory for vertically developed targets is essentially the ballistic path. For bunkers, rooftops, or any other target of horizontal orientation, the GBU-27 flies a commanded pitch down after release to strike the target in as near a vertical attitude as possible. These modes, coupled with the penetrating warhead and excellent accuracy of the weapon, caused the GBU-27 to become the primary F-117A weapon in Desert Storm. While the exact circular error probable (CEP) of the GBU-27 is not presently releasable, the video tape aired during Desert Storm depicts weapons consistently striking the center of the crosshairs .

The most recent maior avionics development is the offensive combat improvement program (OCIP). Based on the WSCS computer system, a number of new systems and capabilities were added. These were color cockpit displays, a digital tactical situation display or moving map, a 4D flight management system (FMS), a new data entry panel, a display processor, autopilot improvements for vertical flight path control, an autothrottle system, and a pilot activated automatic recovery system.

The OCIP program provides no new capabilities for target acquisition and attack. What it does do, is provide the pilot greater situational awareness, reduces pilot workload by allowing the FMS system to fly complex profiles automatically, provides automatic speed and time over target control, and provides unusual attitude recovery upon pilot command.

For the future, a number of major new systems are planned for the aircraft. A new IRADS system is now in production retrofit. Goals for this program are to double the acquisition range of the IRADS system and to increase the range and life of the laser. To replace the aging, out of production SPNGEANS inertial navigation system, a ring laser gyro (RLG) system will be installed. This system will be supplemented by the addition of a global positioning system (GPS) unit.

Although it incorporated many new technolo-

Lockheed Martin

Pilots and boomers claim the F-117A is a relatively easy aircraft to inflight refuel. The F-117A's receptacle meets the RCS spec by rotating closed when not in use. It thus fairs cleanly into the upper surface of the fuselage.

gies, the F-117A, typical of a *Skunk Works* product, was developed in significantly less time and for less cost than a comparable conventional fighter. This was achieved within the tight security of a special access program using streamlined management methods. The Air Force's Aeronautical Systems Division and *Skunk Works* personnel worked in a non-adversarial, problem solving atmosphere with a minimum number of people. In addition, the use of proven components from other aircraft reduced risk and gave the confidence to proceed concurrently with development and low rate production.

Original F-117A program costs can be broken down as follows: Total development to date— $2 billion; Procurement—$4.265 billion (Total flyaway—$2.515 billion; Unit flyaway— $42.6 mil-

lion); Military construction—$295 million; Total program cost—$6.560 billion. These costs include all government furnished equipment, including engines.

PRODUCTION AND OPERATIONAL SERVICE:

The advent of the new aircraft's development and flight test program, under the management of the Air Force's Aeronautical Systems Division, brought with it the added security requirement of communication without identification. Accordingly, similar to other exotic aircraft types flying in the southern Nevada area, an arbitrary radio call of "117" was assigned. This same radio call had been used by the enigmatic 4477th "Red Hats/Red Eagles" unit that often had flown expatriated MiGs in the area, but there was no

Orders to deploy to Saudi Arabia to support what eventually would become Operation Desert Shield and later, Operation Desert Storm, arrived at the 37th TFW's Tonapah headquarters on August 17, 1990. Three days later the unit was on alert in the Middle East . The aircraft are shown during a temporary stopover at Langley AFB, Virginia.

relationship to the call and the formal F-19 designation then being considered by the Air Force. Apparently, use of the "117" radio call became commonplace and when Lockheed released its first flight manual ("dash one"), F-11 7A was the designation imprinted on the cover.

Additionally, though not officially acknowledged, the aircraft has acquired several nicknames. Pilot's and the press have, on occasion, referred to the aircraft as the *Wobbly Goblin* or *Bat Jet*, and there is some indication that the codename *Blue Maria* was utilized. However, the name that has now been formally chosen for the F-117A is *Nighthawk*.

The first production aircraft, 785, was flown on January 15, 1982. With production concur-rence at an average rate of eight aircraft per year, initial operational capability was achieved during October of 1983, only twenty-eight months after the F117A's first flight. The last of fifty-nine aircraft was completed and delivered to the Air Force's Tactical Air Command during June of 1990.

Flight testing of the F-11 7A was undertaken at both Groom Lake and the old WWII-vintage Tonopah Test Range Airfield (elevation, 5,540 ft.) 140 miles northwest of Las Vegas (and Nellis AFB), Nevada and conveniently positioned between the Cactus and Kawich mountain ranges. Located near the old silver mining town of Tonopah and often referred to as TTR (Tonopah Test Range), it had undergone a major refurbishment following a 1981 Air Force decision to move all F-117 operational activity from Groom Lake (though all first flights, following truck delivery from Lockheed, continued to be conducted there). Refurbishment, as part of the original Lockheed contract, included the construction of some 54 hangars, a general runway overhaul including a length increase from 10,000 to 12,500 ft., and accommodations for some 2,500 personnel.

Pilot recruitment for the program primarily was on a volunteer basis. Tours were for three years (this requirement is now being changed to two) and crews were not allowed to bring their families to Tonopah (instead, they were forced to find accommodations for them in nearby desert towns or in Las Vegas, proper—while commuting between home and base via contract transport aircraft--usually Key Airline). Minimum flight time required as pilot-in-command was 1,000 hours. Initial training took place in Vought A-7Ds (during 1989, concurrent with the formation of the 37th TFW, these were replaced by Northrop T-38As and AT-38As) during daylight flights, and this was followed by preliminary hops out to a radius of 200 miles from Tonopah in the F-11 7A at night. As proficiency increased, longer flights were undertaken, until the pilot was declared both proficient and combat ready. To date, the longest missions known to have been flown in the F-117 have lasted some 12 hours with inflight refueling. Present practice sortie rates result in pilots logging 15 to 20 hours per month in the F-117A and another 5 or 6 hours per month in the AT-38.

The first operational-standard production aircraft was turned over to the Tactical Air Command's 4450th Tactical Group during 1982, and on October 26, 1983, initial operational capability (IOC) was attained (with the 415th TFS; the 416th followed during January). The group initially was a direct reporting unit to the Tactical Air Command, Langley AFB, Virginia. During 1985, however, operational command was transferred to the Tactical Fighter Weapons Center, Nellis, AFB, Nevada. During October of 1989, it became the 37th Tactical Fighter Wing (under the operational command of the 12th Air Force, headquartered at Bergstrom AFB, Texas) comprised of the 415th and 416th Tactical Fighter Squadrons, and the 417th Tactical Fighter Training Squadron.

The 37th has now given up its aircraft to the 49th TFW and the unit has been moved from Tonopah to Holloman AFB, New Mexico. This took

The F-117A's weapon bay is capable of accommodating up to 5,000 pounds of bombs . The GBU-27 is a 2,000 pound bomb coupled to a Paveway 3 laser energy seeker.

Leaflets, such as this one, dropped from aircraft were used extensively during Operation Desert Storm to warn the civilian populace of impending disaster. This leaflet stated simply, "Leave, this place is going to be bombed".

"Warning. This place is going to be bombed. Leave all your belongings and flee to save your life. Warning."

place during the spring of 1992. Holloman has lost the 479th Tactical Training Wing which operated111 Northrop T-38A/AT-38B aircraft. Weather, traffic, and airspace availability have been cited as reasons for the move. However, accessibility to the White Sands Missile Range and McGregor, Oscura, Beak, and Talon ranges for training were important factors. Following the move, Tonopah became a deployment site for Red Flag.

Prior to public acknowledgement of the aircraft by the Department of Defense during November of 1988, all information pertaining to its existence and activities was denied. All flight operations from Tonopah were conducted at night, and special precautions, such as keeping the aircraft hangarbound until 30 minutes after sunset, and conducting ground operations in blacked-out conditions, were standard.

Because of these constraints, pilot workloads (which sometimes involved two flights a night) were considered inordinately high and there were problems. Complaints concerning spatial disorientation and fatigue were not uncommon, and at least two of three acknowledged accidents were thought to have been attributable to related difficulties. The first production aircraft crashed on June 21, 1982 during a test flight on the Nellis range (the Lockheed pilot survived). Later, two other aircraft crashed, these including 81-0792 on July 11, 1986 15 n. miles northeast of Bakersfield, California, and 83-0815 on October 14, 1987, on the Nellis range. In both of the latter accidents the Air Force pilots, Maj. Ross E. Mulhare and Maj. Michael C. Stewart, respectively, were killed.

On the plus side, the 37th TFW already has been recognized for its distinguished service and accomplishments. Top performance has earned it superior ratings during Operational Readiness Inspections. During 1988, the 4450th TG was awarded the TAC Commander's Maintenance Award in the Special Mission category. During 1989, the Air Force Association honored the F-117A program with its "Most Outstanding Service to National Defense in Manned Flight" award. Perhaps most significantly, during the same year, the prestigious Collier Trophy for "The Greatest Achievement in Aeronautics or Astronautics in America" was presented to "Ben R. Rich and the entire Lockheed/Air Force team for the production and deployment of the F-117A stealth aircraft which changes the entire concept of military aircraft design and combat deployment for the future".

Daylight proficiency was not ignored during this period and accommodating this were missions in Vought A-7Ds assigned to the 4450th. Tailcoded LV, these aircraft were standard Corsair IIs and, contrary to popular impression, were not specially modified in any way. On several occasions, the A-7Ds were spotted "out of country"—most notably in England. The A-7Ds, as mentioned previously, were replaced by T-38s during 1989. Additionally, it should be noted that an exchange program with the F-117A exists and that at least one Royal Air Force pilot has been involved.

Since assuming the stealth mission, the 37th TFW has twice taken part in combat operations. The wing's F-117As led the attack against Panama on December 21, 1989 during Operation Just Cause. Pinpoint bombing stunned and disrupted the Panamanian infantry at Rio Hato and paved the way for US paratroopers to land and eventually overcome the Panamanian opposition. This operation, though successful, did not test the aircraft from a low-observables standpoint as Panama had no radar defense network.

The F-117's second combat tour began on August 17, 1990 when the 37th TFW received its deployment order to Saudi Arabia for Operation Desert Shield. On August 21, eighteen F-117As from the 37th's 415th Tactical Fighter Squadron (TFS) arrived at King Khalid Air Base. These aircraft had departed from Tonapah on August 19 and after a brief stop enroute at Langley AFB, Virginia, had continued on to Saudi Arabia.

On August 23, the 415th TFS launched eight orientation sorties with the Saudis. Three days later, the F-117A assumed alert duty for the first time in its history.

On December 3, eighteen F-117As from the second 37th TFW squadron, the 416th TFS, deployed to King Khalid Air Base from Langley AFB. They arrived at their destination the following day.

The following several weeks were spent involved in various training exercises and bringing the unit up to full operational readiness. In the meantime, the international political situation involving the confrontation between Iraq and the US continued to deteriorate. On January 16, the 37th TFWP (now Tactical Fighter Wing Provisional for purposes of alignment with other coalition forces) received orders to execute its D-day tasking against targets in Iraq; however, the first wave of F-1 17As did not depart on their first combat mission until after midnight.

Twenty-two minutes after midnight, on January 17, ten F-117As from the 415th TFS launched against a combined integrated operations center/ground control intercept site at Nukhayb, two air defense control sector headquarters facilities, and the Iraqi Air Force Headquarters building in Baghdad, a joint integrated operations center/radar facility at Al Taqaddum, a telephone center at Ar Ramadi and two in Baghdad, an integrated operations center at Al Taji, a North Taji military related facility, and

An F-117A is shown with Lockheed YF-22A, N22YX, probably at Palmdale, California. Size and weight of the two aircraft are roughly comparable. Even more amazing is the fact the two aircraft represent two basically dissimilar approaches to RCS technology and are at least one generation apart.

F-117A refueling receptacle is located on-center on the aircraft dorsal spine. It is a rotating assembly that does not require separate doors for sealing. Noteworthy are the extended UHF antenna and the rotating beacon. Also noteworthy are the assymetrically displaced pitot assemblies.

*Profile view of **F-117A, 830,** of the 416th TFS. Visible along with the forward, ventrally mounted UHF communication antenna (left) are the two tube-like ventral radar reflectors (right). The latter, along with the faceted dorsal reflectors, are easily removed and are used only during peacetime operations.*

*Security concerning the **F-117,** its mission, and its technology remains extremely tight, as of this writing, as evidenced by the two armed guards protecting **828** during its 1990 visit to Carswell AFB. Noteworthy is the serial number visible on the lower portion of the nose gear strut assembly.*

The first F-117A, No. 780, today can be seen as a gate guardian near the entrance to Nellis AFB, Nevada. The second full-scale development aircraft, No. 781, is now displayed at the Air Force Museum, Wright-Patterson AFB, Ohio.

the Presidential grounds at Abu Ghurayb.

A second wave of twelve F-117As (three from the 415th and nine from the 416th) left shortly afterwards to repeat strikes against the Iraqi Air Force Headquarters, air defense sector headquarters, and telephone exchanges in Baghdad; the Alo Taqaddum integrated operations center/ground control intercept facility; military related facilities at North Taji, and the Presidential grounds at Abu Ghurayb. New targets included the Salmon Pak troposcatter station; a television transmitter station, international radio transmitter, and the Presidential bunker in Baghdad; Rasheed Airfield; a joint integrated operations center/ground control intercept site at Ar Rutbah; a troposcatter station at Habbaniyah; and the communications satellite terminal at Ad Dujayl.

On January 25, 1991, six more F-117As flew from Langley AFB to King Khalid Air Base, where they were assigned to the 416th TFS. Their arrival resulted in a total contingent of 42 combat ready F-117As.

Operation Desert Storm thus became the first combat environment wherein the F-1 17A was utilized in a real-world test against a modern, integrated air defense. The *Nighthawks* of the 37th TFW repeatedly flew into and through intense anti-aircraft artillery and surface-to-air missile fire, accurately delivering 2,000 tons of precision-guided munitions during 1,300 combat sorties. Wing pilots scored 1,600 direct hits against enemy targets in nearly 400 locations. Without suffering a single loss, or experiencing any damage, they destroyed hardened command and control bunkers, aircraft shelters, production and storage facilities for nuclear, biological, and chemical weapons, and other heavily defended targets of

the highest military and political significance.

Employing just 2.5% of the Air Force assets in theater, the 37th TFW not only led the UN coalition force against Iraq, but also hit nearly 40% of the Iraqi targets that came under fire in the first three days. Twenty-nine F117As hit twenty-six high value targets on the first night alone. The F-117As were so effective that the Iraqi air defense system virtually collapsed. Iraq's command, control, and communications network never recovered.

Thereafter, the 37th TFW constantly hit key political and military targets to further weaken Iraqi resistance and to prepare for the ground campaign. Early on, and employing only four F-117As, Baghdad's nuclear research facility was attacked, completely destroying its three reactor cores. Noteworthy is the fact the F-117s were the only coalition aircraft tasked to fly over Baghdad during the entire Desert Storm operation.

During another strike, the 37th TFW destroyed a whole network of surface-to-air missile sites in central Iraq in the space of one hour, thus enabling B-52s to carpet-bomb Republican Guard positions without fear of interception. Immediately prior to the start of the coalition's ground campaign, the F-117A destroyed a complex of pumping stations and; distribution network that fed oil into anti-person nel fire trenches in southern Kuwait. Thl attack earned strong praise and the gratitude of the multinational ground forces.

At 0015 hours on February 28, 1991, th 37th TFWP received good news: all operations relating to *Desert Storm* combat were suspend ed in order to give the Iraqis an opportunity t sign a cease fire agreement. Combat for th 37th TFWP had come

to an end.

Statistically, during the course of *Desert Storm*, the 37th TFW compiled a record that is unparalleled in the chronicles of air warfare. The *Nighthawks* achieved a 80% hit rate on pinpoint targets (1,669 direct hits and 418 misses) while destroying nearly 40% of all strategic targets attacked by the coalition forces.

The 37th TFW's performance also drew high praise from military and political leaders. In particular, Senator Sam Nunn, Senate Armed Services Committee Chairman, stated, the F-117A to be "the heart of our offensive power and targeting capability." Brigadier General "Buster" Glossen, Fourteenth Air Division Commander, called the 37th TFW "the backbone of the strategic air campaign." General Colin Powell, Chairman of the Joint Chiefs of Staff, commented, "You are showing the nation what it's all about—the combination of the very highest technology with the very best kind of people we can put together in the field as a team." Secretary of Defense Richard Cheney stated, "You have gone far beyond anything anybody envisioned...it has been phenomenal."

The F-117A has been placed on alert status on at least two other occasions. An anti-terrorist raid was planned but later cancelled against Libya during April of 1986, and a similar attack against Syria also was planned and cancelled in retaliation for the 1983 bombing of the marine barracks in Lebanon. In both instances, there is some possibility that reported temporary relocating of at least two F-117As to bases in England was undertaken to accommodate such missions.

The Air Force's F-117As presently are supported by the Sacramento Air Logistics Center at McClellan AFB, California. This unit has established a depot at Air Force Plant 42 in Palmdale, California (also the location of Northrop B-2 final assembly) specifically to accommodate forthcoming F-117A overhaul requirements. At a nearby facility, also on the Palmdale airport, Lockheed maintains an update facility where F-117A systems are continuously upgraded to maintain technological currency.

As of mid-1995, Air Force units assigned the F-117 are as follows:

Testing (Code ED), 412th OG, 410th FLTS, Palmdale, California

49th Fighter Wing, Holloman AFB, New Mexico consists of 49th OG with 7th FS (Code HO and named *Bunys*), 8th FS (Code HO and named *The Black Sheep*), 9th FS (Code HO and named *The Iron Knights*)

57th TG, 422nd TES, DET 1, Holloman AFB, New Mexico (Code WA)

Sacramento Air Maintenance & Overhaul Logistics Center, McClellan AFB, California, 77th ABW, 337th FLTS

F-117 serial numbers originally were assumed to be allocated on a contract year basis in conformity with known Department of Defense standards. This information since has been found to be inaccurate, and accordingly, has been revised and brought up to date as follows:

	No.	Comment:
F-117A	780	FSD aircraft now displayed at Nellis AFB
F-117A	781	FSD aircraft now displayed at USAF Museum; arrived there on July 17, 1991
F-117A	782	FSD aircraft
F-117A	783	FSD aircraft
F-117A	784	FSD aircraft
F-117A	785	Written-off April 20, 1982 prior to Air Force accep tance; first production aircraft

One of the first images released by Lockheed of what originally was referred to as the F-117N. This is a Navy-dedicated configuration with revised wing leading and trailing edge sweep and many concessions to carrier landing requirements.

F-117A	786
F-117A	787
F-117A	788
F-117A	789
F-117A	790
F-117A	791
F-117A	792
F-117A	793
F-117A	794
F-117A	795
F-117A	796
F-117A	797
F-117A	798
F-117A	799
F-117A	800
F-117A	801	Written-off August 4, 1992
F-117A	802
F-117A	803
F-117A	804
F-117A	805
F-117A	806
F-117A	807
F-117A	808
F-117A	809
F-117A	810
F-117A	811
F-117A	812
F-117A	813
F-117A	814
F-117A	815	Written-off October 14, 1987
F-117A	816
F-117A	817
F-117A	818
F-117A	819
F-117A	820
F-117A	821
F-117A	822
F-117A	823
F-117A	824
F-117A	825
F-117A	826
F-117A	827
F-117A	828
F-117A	829
F-117A	830
F-117A	831	Flight test aircraft
F-117A	832

Another view of an early navalized F-117 configuration. As originally unveiled to the public, the aircraft was referred to as the F-117N. Today, in slightly modified form, it is referred to by Lockheed as the A/F-117X.

F-117A	833
F-117A	834
F-117A	835
F-117A	836
F-117A	837
F-117A	838
F-117A	839
F-117A	840
F-117A	841
F-117A	842
F-117A	843	Last production aircraft; delivered July 12, 1990

FUTURE DEVELOPMENT:

A/F-117X Attack Aircraft—Initially referred to as the F-117N, the A/F-117X is an upgraded and improved Navy derivative of the original F-117A. The basic F-117A structure has been retained, requiring only increased strength materials to meet the operating environment needed by a carrier-borne aircraft. The F-117A already possesses three primary Navy characteristics not normally found in Air Force aircraft. These are: a full-depth center line keel from nose gear to tail hook; three full-depth fuselage frames for wing carry through; and the main landing gear being attached directly to a major bulkhead. These features allow maximum utilization of existing F-117A tooling. This results in lower program cost and lower associated risk.

Carrier suitable aerodynamic qualities are achieved through the integration of a larger, reduced-sweep wing and the addition of horizontal tail surfaces. The fuselage is unchanged from the Air Force design with the exception of the canopy configuration and ventral weapons bay fairing. All aerodynamic modifications are

Latest navalized F-117 study released by Lockheed is the A/F-117X. This aircraft is equipped with folding wings, additional horizontal tail surfaces for improved low-speed pitch control, revised engine exhaust nozzles, a tailhook, heavy-duty landing gear, a redesigned nose, a new canopy providing improved visibility, and other changes.

F-117A, 82-0807, at Tonopah Test Range facility near Tonopah, Nevada. Base is located approximately 140 miles northwest of Las Vegas, Nevada next to the town of Tonopah. Contrary to the image presented, this and other static views of the F-117A were taken by Lockheed photographer Eric Schulzinger in sub-zero temperatures.

Direct head-on view of *F-117A, 82-0807,* at Tonopah Test Range facility. Extreme angularity of paneling in nose section is heavily accented. Offset red rotating beacon (one of two; the other is located dorsally) is visible on the starboard underside of the aircraft. Noteworthy are three-digits of serial number painted on nose gear strut.

Inflight view of *F-117A, 81-0796,* over what appear to be the Sierra Madre mountains of California. Extended UHF antenna and bolt-on red rotating beacon are noteworthy. Other antennas are mounted ventrally and are similarly retractable. Noteworthy also are the so-called 'platypus' exhaust nozzles.

*Another view of **F-117A, 82-0807,** at Tonopah Test Range. Angled position of landing gear door is unusual, but it compensates for slight inward retraction angle of main gear as it swings forward and up into well. Gold coloring of canopy transparencies is readily discernible, as is gold screen material protecting FLIR/laser designator unit.*

*An unidentified **F-117A** receives fuel from McDonnell Douglas KC-10A, 82-0191, of the 22nd ARW. F-117A refueling receptacle is located aft of the canopy, thus complicating piloting requirements. Receptacle apparently is integral with rotating door assembly. Night refueling requires use of small light at apex of canopy framing.*

LOCKHEED MARTIN F-117A
NIGHTHAWK

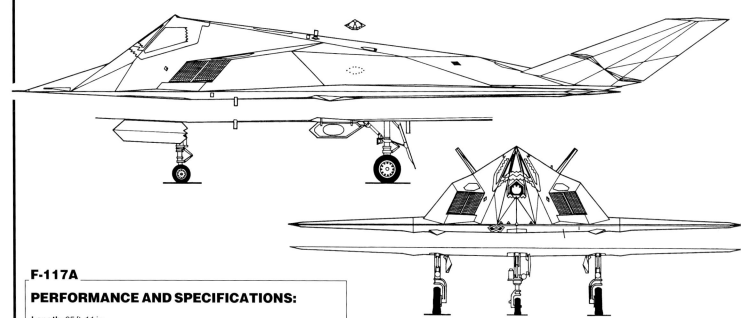

F-117A

PERFORMANCE AND SPECIFICATIONS:

Length: 65 ft. 11 in.
Wingspan: 43 ft. 4 in.
Wing Area: 913 sq. ft.
Height: 12 ft. 5 in.
Empty Wt.: 29,500 pounds
Max. Gross Takeoff Weight: 52,500 pounds
Maximum Speed: .90 Mach/603 mph @ 35,000 ft.
Operational Ceiling: 52,000 ft.
Max. Unrefueled Range: 1,250 mi. (internal fuel)
Fixed Armament: various free-falling and laser guided weapons
Powerplant: 2 x 10,800 pound thrust General Electric F404-GE-F1D2 low bypass ratio turbofans

Have Blue

PERFORMANCE AND SPECIFICATIONS:

Length: 47 ft. 3 in.
Wingspan: 22 ft. 8 in.
Wing Area: 386 sq. ft.
Height: 7 ft. 6-1/2 in.
Empty Wt.: 8,950 pounds
Max. Gross Takeoff Weight: 12,500 pounds
Maximum Speed: .80 Mach/536 mph @ 35,000 ft.
Operational Ceiling: unknown
Max. Unrefueled Endurance: 1 hour (internal fuel)
Powerplant: 2 x 2,950 pound thrust General Electric J85-GE-4A axial flow turbojets

LOCKHEED *HAVE BLUE*

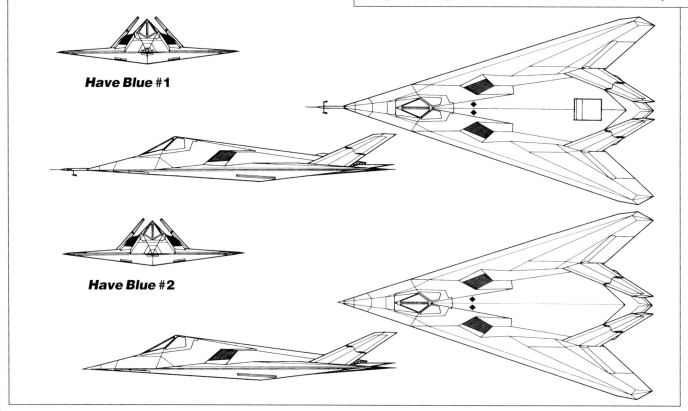

Have Blue #1

Have Blue #2

F-117A MARKINGS:

Operational F-117As are painted flat black. The paint covers the RAM panels which are said to have a normally medium gray surface color of their own. The base color of the natural aluminum aircraft without RAM panels is apparently a white epoxy paint that improves the glue grip of the epoxy formula used as an adhesive for the RAM panels. The white paint sometimes is visible when RAM panels break, chip, or crack. White, heat absorbing tiles (usually painted black to blend with the rest of the aircraft) are attached to the extended exhaust lip just aft of the flat exhaust openings. All three landing gear wells, the landing gear struts, wheels, and related assemblies are all painted in white epoxy. The faired tailhook well is outlined in red. Most of the retractable communications and navigation system antennas are painted white. The national insigne, Tactical Air Command badge, miscellaneous tail markings (including the three digits of the assigned serial number), "no step" stencils, and other miscellany are painted medium gray (F.S. 36118). Crew names, when applied, are painted just under the cockpit sill in white. The ejection seat triangle and rescue block, when applied, are flat red. The cockpit is generally painted in black and gray. The instrument panel combing is in black and the ACES II ejection seat is gray. Other cockpit colors are conventional. Some aircraft have been seen with the 4450th TG badge painted in gray and flat red on the intake cheek areas. More recently marked aircraft carry the 37th TFW badge in the same position. At least one aircraft carried a painted U.S. flag on the underside of the fuselage; the forward triangle created by the nose (moving aft to just behind the nose gear well) was blue with white stars, and the red and white stripes flared aft, widening until they contacted the wing trailing edge. Another F-117 had a large black skunk against a white circle background painted on its undersurface.

WEAPON OPTIONS:

To date, the following weapons have been seen being carried by the F-117A: GBU-27; GBU-24; GBU-I5; GBU-10; and both infrared and laser-guided versions of the AGM-65 Maverick. There is some indication, also, that the aircraft has a limited air-to-air capability with AIM-9 Sidewinders and the AIM-120 and that it can carry any of several different nuclear weapons.

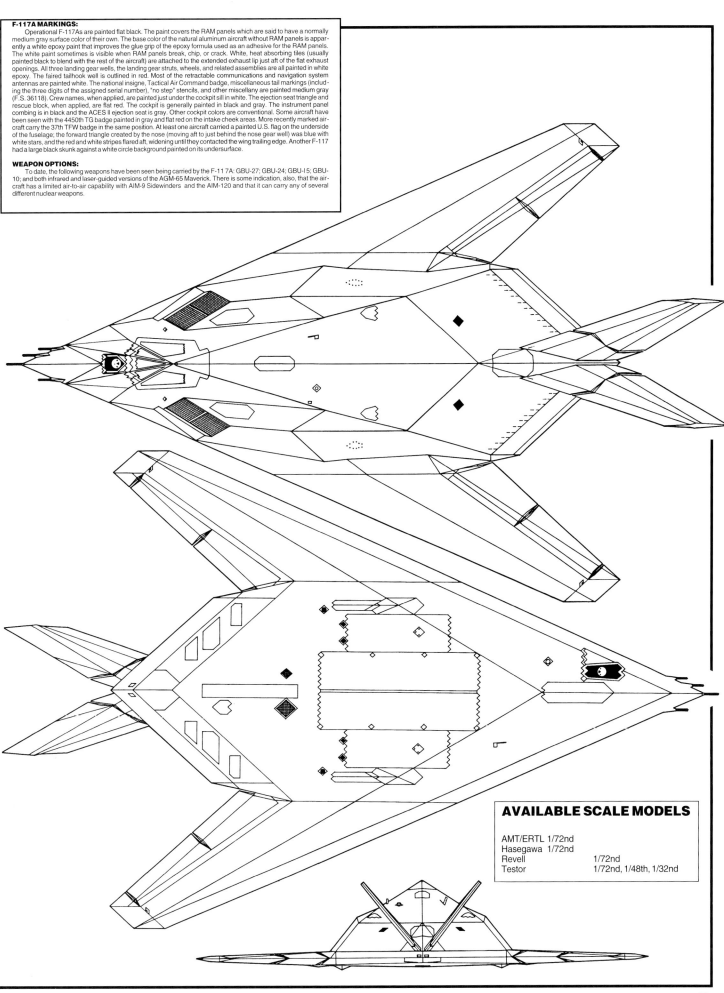

AVAILABLE SCALE MODELS

AMT/ERTL 1/72nd	
Hasegawa 1/72nd	
Revell	1/72nd
Testor	1/72nd, 1/48th, 1/32nd

Jay Miller/Aerofax, Inc.

The view into the cockpit from the outside is effectively undisturbed by gold film laminate. Visible is HUD, HUD panel, and main instrument panel port CRT. Basic panel consists of two small CRTs surrounding a larger, central unit. Panel coloring is generally black. Other interior colors appear to consist of conventional grays.

Jay Miller/Aerofax, Inc.

Lockheed **F-117A, 80-0790,** shortly after its arrival at Nellis AFB, Nevada on April 21, 1990. This was the aircraft's first public showing. By the time of photo, all antennas had been retracted. Drag chute compartment doors remain open, however. Markings were specially applied for this event.

Jay Miller/Aerofax, Inc.

Lockheed **F-117A, 84-0828,** shortly ater its arrival at Nellis AFB, Nevada on April 21, 1990. Aircraft's 37th TFW markings, visible on the vertical tail, were specially applied for this event, as were the TR tailcode and related items. F-117As normally are flown only with serial numbers and national insignia visible.

Nose section markings are minimal. All are in white. Unusually, the ejection seat triangle also is in white. Coloration of gold film laminate in canopy transparencies is readily apparent. A similar effect can be seen on the intake and FLIR/DLIR/laser screens at certain angles.

*Empennage of **F-117A** is complex interfacing of several different planes. Airfoil section of V-tail surfaces is totally unorthodox. Somewhat jagged edge to upswept trailing edge lip is noteworthy. Visible lower left is red outline of tailhook compartment. Also visible is gray accent to white lettering.*

The proposed A/F-117X will be capable of self-defense when carrying AIM-9 and AIM-120 variants in its extended and enlarged ventral weapon bay. Weapon payload capacity will be increased from 5,000 to 10,000 pounds.

achievable with no degradation to existing signature levels. Survivability will actually improve in many areas. F-117A landing gear are replaced with modified F-14 landing gear reducing development costs and increasing commonalty with rolling stock already in inventory aboard carriers.

As stated previously, the A/F-117X leverages significantly off of the investment already made in the F-117A. Avionics are relatively unchanged, requiring only the addition of an off-the-shelf automatic carrier landing system (ACLS). Propulsion system integration, all major subsystems, application of low observable technology, the air data system, the precision weapon delivery system, and all primary aircraft software are all drawn from the F-117A...resulting in a quick, efficient and affordable development program.

With the retirement of the Grumman A-6 fleet during 1999, the Navy will lose the capability to place regional trouble spots at risk from the sea. Modification to existing conventional aircraft or increased use of the *Tomahawk* cruise missile will not guarantee target destruction with minimum collateral damage. Stealth and precision, will. The A/F-117X can provide these requisite capabilities and can do so until the definitive AX—the replacement for the A-6—becomes operational some seventeen years from now.

The A/F-117X has gone through a number of design studies alongside the Air Force's F-117A+ and F-117B. Each of these has been configured to accommodate a specific tactical need. The F-117A+ was a proposed modification of existing Air Force aircraft that would have led to the incorporation of 18 advanced low-observables technologies and other improvements. The current A/F-117X for the Navy, for which the Senate Armed Services Committee has earmarked $175 million to initiate a program definition phase and flying demonstrator, would involve new production aircraft. It would feature a beefed-up fuselage to accommodate carrier landings, a folding wing, a carrier-qualified tailhook, and access to equipment weapons bays with "tail over water" and/or one engine running. Flyaway cost was estimated to be $76 million per aircraft in 1994, based on a 100 aircraft production run.

The F-117B, which like the A/F-117X would involve new production aircraft, would capitalize on commonalty with the A/F-117X while leveraging the investment made in the F-117A. The result would be a superior attack aircraft with a higher maximum gross takeoff weight than the F-117A (73,200 pounds v/s 52,500 pounds), an increased combat radius (980 n. miles v/s 570 n. miles), and double the internal payload (10,000 pounds v/s 5,000 pounds). The Navy's A/F-117X would have a wing with a reduced sweep angle of 42°, a span increased by 21.45 ft., and a new tail (conventional horizontal tail surfaces would be added).

A new wing also would give the F-117B a distinct shape and all-weather sensors, advanced signature characteristics, improved aerodynamics, and twin General Electric F414 afterburning turbofan engines would press the state-of-the-art for low-observable aircraft.

In a push for modular production and further cost savings, LMADC is proposing the Navy and Air Force execute a joint program to build both the A/F-117X and the F-117B together. Common hardware would include fuselage, engines, inlet, nozzle, and horizontal and vertical tails. The aircraft would differ in some individual components such as landing gear and select avionics.

A five-year modification program to improve the standard F-117A was completed during mid-1995. This program, under a $250 million Air Force contract, began in 1990 when aircraft "805" arrived at Palmdale. The retrofit involved integration of an expanded computer memory and throughput with state-of-the-art avionics to significantly improve pilot situational awareness and reduce pilot workload. The upgrade enhances mission effectiveness by allowing the pilot to focus on target acquisition and weapons delivery while the F-117A flies its complex profiles automatically. Automatic time control throughout the flight ensures time-over-target and bomb impact within one second of what is planned. Another feature gives pilots the ability to command automatic recovery from unsafe attitudes. It is the first use of four-dimensional flight management and automatic recovery in any Air Force tactical fighter.

Lockheed Martin briefed the British Ministry of Defence on a proposed derivative of the Air Force's F-117B during July of 1995. It is being suggested to meet the Staff Target (Air) 425 deep-strike requirement that will otherwise remain unfulfilled when the RAF's Panavia *Tornado* GR4s are retired by the end of this century. In order to accommodate political issues, the proposed RAF variant would have GEC-Marconi-supplied avionics, Eurojet EJ200 engines, and some structural content indigenous to Great Britain in the form of structure produced by British Aerospace.

On a final note, the name *Nighthawk* was officially adopted for the F-117 during 1994.

CONSTRUCTION AND SYSTEMS:

Fuselage: Conventional aluminum construction with plate-like RAM attached externally via epoxy adhesive. Quadruple-redundant fly-by-wire flight control system is fed environmental data via four RCS-optimized composite construction pitot assemblies mounted on nose. Two pitots are mounted on the starboard side, one is mounted centrally, and the remaining unit is mounted on the port side. All communications, EW, and other antennas and protuberances are either retractable or removeable. Optional radar reflector assembly and night flying lights can be bolted to the outside of each engine nacelle when non-combat operations in a civilian environment are required.

Cockpit: Conventional single-seat configuration with McDonnell Douglas ACES II. (Advanced Capability Ejection Seat) ejection seat under a single-piece, hydraulically-actuated, aft-hinged, five-transparency canopy. Environmental control system identical to that utilized in Lockheed C-130. Communications radios and Honeywell inertial navigation system common to other aircraft. Sophisticated navigation/attack system is integrated with avionics suite. Displays consist of main central CRT on front panel and two peripheral smaller CRTs; minimal analog instrumentation primarily emergency back-up. Controls are conventional with centrally-mounted stick and rudder pedals interfaced with F-16-type quadruple redundant fly-by-wire system. Conventional, non-Raster heads-up-display is mounted above instrument panel combing.

Canopy transparencies are laminated and incorporate a gold film coating specifically optimized to lower radar returns from the cockpit. Additionally, the panels around the canopy area are given serrated edges to reflect energy at angles away from the beaming radar's receiver. The canopy weighs approximately 400 pounds.

Though not integral with the cockpit, it should be noted that detailed planning for missions into heavily defended target areas is accomplished by an automated mission planning system developed specifically to optimize the F-117A's capabilities.

Wings: Conventional aluminum construction materials with slab surfaces optimized to conform to computer-generated RCS specification. RAM materials applied in sheet form with smaller areas spray-covered. Conventional hydraulically-

In consideration of the fact it will be required to operate on and off of aircraft carriers, the proposed navalized F-117 will be equipped with a variety of high-lift devides including an extensive trailing edge flap system and associated spoilers.

boosted elevons for pitch/roll control and hydro-mechanically actuated flaperons are fitted. W-shaped trailing edge design is optimized to conform to RCS equations. Wings are removable, but only with significant effort. Rumors pertaining to F-117A common transportability via C-5A/B remain unverified, but regardless, wing disassembly is not optimized for quick turnaround. Fuel tanks are integral with design.

Tail Surfaces: V-type design with double diamond airfoil optimized for low RCS. Thermoplastic graphite composites are the primary construction material (original surfaces on production aircraft were of aluminum). Covered with RAM. Prism-like cross-section. Hydraulically-actuated slab surfaces work in yaw mode only and do not contribute to pitch control.

Landing Gear: Heavy-duty conventional tri-cycle oleo-pneumatic configuration. Gear retraction direction is forward with all three gear assemblies Main gear have a slight inward angular motion during the retraction process. All three gear wells are covered with prism-type RAM-surfaced doors that are hydraulically assisted during the closing process in order to assure tight fit. Bendix carbon heat-sink brakes are the same as those utilized on the McDonnell Douglas F-15. Anti-skid is integral with brake system. A special all-black, ring type drag chute and associated housing (with split cover doors) are mounted in the empennage area between the vertical tail surfaces. An arresting hook for use in emergencies is ventrally mounted in an enclosed well under empennage.

Powerplant: Two General Electric F404-GE F1 D2 two-shaft, augmented low-bypass-ratio turbofans. Engines are not afterburner equipped but generally are similar to other F404s in configuration and installation. Fan is three-stage type with a bypass ratio of 0.34. Airflow is 142 lbs./sec. (64 kg.). The high-pressure compressor is a seven stage unit with an over-all pressure ratio of 25:1 The combustion chamber is a single-piece annular design. The high-pressure turbine is a single-stage unit with air-cooled blades. The low-pressure turbine is also a single-stage unit. Maximum diameter is 34.8 in. (880 mm). Maximum sea level thrust rating is 10,800 lbs. Oversize intake with structural splitter assembly has an electrically de-iced composite construction grid with a roughly 3/4" x 1-1/2" cell dimension. This serves to deflect incoming (10 centimeter wavelength/3GHz/E-band-radar-generated energy away from the highly reflective engine compressor section first stage turbine blades. The "platypus" exhaust duct assembly is an extremely wide slot (approx. 62 in.) with an extended and upward-angled lower lip. It is optimized to spread the exhaust plume and increase the rapidity of the ambient cool air mix. The lower lip serves to reduce the angular viewing window into the exhaust proper. This lip not only lowers aft quadrant RCS, but also contributes to lowering of the aircraft IR signature. The vaned exhaust nozzle system has 12 slots on each side. A large, down-ward-folding-auxiliary inlet door is located on top of each engine nacelle. Fuel consumption from "wet" wing tanks at cruise speed and altitude is approximately 3,000 lbs. an hour. Fuel capacity is approximately 1,850 gals. and fuel type is conventional JP-4. Aircraft is inflight refuelable with a rotating dorsally-mounted receiver aft of cockpit area and between engine bays. Refueling receptacle is illuminated for night operations by small floodlight mounted at apex of canopy dome assembly and is covered by a single door.

Weapons/Sensors: Forward-looking Texas Instruments IR and downward-looking IR sensors are mounted separately with former permanently affixed behind an IR-transparent covering just ahead of and below the windscreen and the latter mounted under the fuselage (on its starboard side) behind another fixed transparency. Laser tracker/designator is mounted in same compartments and is integral with FLIR/DLIR. Weapon bay with dual hinged, hydraulically actuated doors is capable of accommodating up to 5,000 lbs. Normal maximum payload complement is two 2,000 lb. bombs though single-bomb payloads

F-117 cockpit is relatively conventional and utilizes components from the McDonnell Douglas F/A-18 and to a lesser degree, other contemporary U.S. fighters. Multi-function display screens provide plethora of data during combat.

are common. Most weapons are of the laser-guided variety and include bombs, missiles, and nuclear weapons. A small family of F-11 7-dedicated weapons with improved accuracy and possibly some stealth features has been developed, but no information is available. Some reports indicate that air-to-air capabilities have been explored.

PRINCIPLES OF RADAR OPERATION:

The external appearance of a radar unit is dominated by its antenna which in most radars is some form of articulated parabolic reflector. The radar antenna can also be a fixed array of many small radiating elements (sometimes in the thousands) operating in unison to produce the desired radiation characteristics. Array antennas have the advantage of greater flexibility and more rapid beam steering than mechanically-steered reflector antennas because the beam movement can be accomplished by electrically changing the relative phase at each element of the antenna. High power can be radiated since a separate transmitter can be applied at each element. Additionally, the flexibility and speed of an array antenna make it necessary in some instances to control its func-

tion and analyze its output by automatic data processing equipment rather than more simple formats involving display devices.

Radars generally operate within the microwave portion of the electromagnetic spectrum, typically from around 200 MHz (1.5 meters wavelength) to around 35,000 MHz (8.5 millimeters wavelength)—though there are a decidedly large number of exceptions. Military radar systems can basically be broken down into three groups: (1) Indirect Threat Radars; (2) Direct Threat Radars; and (3) Non-Threat Radars. Each of these consists of the following:

Indirect Threat:
Early Warning (EW) or Long Range Radar (LRR)—is a high-power set used for long range detection of aircraft. Its main purpose is early detection as opposed to accuracy. Hence it is characterized by relatively long pulse widths (2 to 20 microseconds), low PRF (100 to 400 pulses per second), and frequencies in the range of 200 to 1,400 mHz. The long PWs allow the transmission of very high power (1 to 10 megaWatts). The low PRF allows very long listening times and ranges up to 300 nm are common.

The scan type used with early warning radars is circular. A narrow fan-shaped beam is

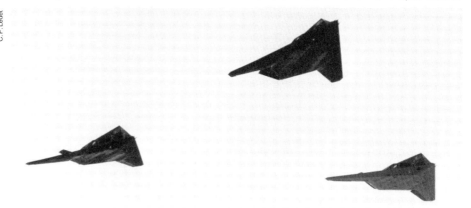

Three F-117As in formation flight over Edwards AFB during 1993. Nighthawk operational missions are usually flown with each aircraft acting as an autonomous unit.

Randy Jolly

*Though early revelations indicated that all markings would be removed from **F-117s** in combat, imagery eminating from the early stages of the Gulf war quickly refuted that. Col. Tony Tolin's well-known **828,** seen at Carswell AFB, bears standard markings for type.*

Randy Jolly

*Application of RAM on **F-117A, 830,** flown by Capt. Chuck Link, bears witness to the fact that it periodically is removed and replaced in large sections. In this view, it appears that 830 has a minor left wing fuel tank leak and that the tank has been accessed on at least one earlier occasion.*

37th Tactical Fighter
Wing patch.

416th Tactical Fighter
Squadron patch.

417th Tactical Fighter Training
Squadron patch.

415th Tactical Fighter
Squadron patch.

"Grim Reapers" patch.

Stepped lower intake lip assembly contains deicing wiper assembly that permits physical removal of ice accumulations in known icing conditions. FLIR ball, with
sensors rotated aft, is readily visible behind protective mesh-like screen assembly just ahead of windscreen. A DLIR is mounted ventrally.

rotated a full circle around a fixed vertical axis. Typically the beam can be shaped to about 2° of azimuth and 10° in elevation. This gives acceptable azimuth resolution and good altitude coverage. This fan-shaped beam is rotated slowly usually three to five rpm so that several successive pulses will hit and reflect from each target. Thus the data collection capability is limited by the PRF and the scan rate.

Acquisition Radar—is associated with ground weapon systems such as anti-aircraft artillery (AAA) or surface-to-air missiles (SAMs) and is a variation of the early warning radar. It is similar in fuction to the EW in that it provides range and azimuth information. This information is used as preliminary information for the target tracking radar. Range resolution is improved as is the azimuth resolution and data collection rate. These radars have shorter PWs (typically one microsecond), PRFs a little higher (perhaps 500 to 800 pulses per second), and more narrow beam widths. In addition, the sweep rate is increased to around 12 rpm. Of course, with the improvement in accuracy comes a sacrifice in range and total power. The maximum theoretical range drops to around 150 nm and the actual ranges are even less because of the power shortfall. These radars normally operate at high frequencies (2,700 to 3,500 mHz) to facilitate focusing of the beam into a more precise pattern.

Height Finder Radars (HF)—The EW, Acquisition, and ASR provide azimuth and range information. One vital intercept parameter is missing with these units, however, and that's altitude. The HF radar supplies this information. It is similar in many respects to the EW radar except that the beam shape and scan type must be modified to provide a narrow beam (typically 1.5°) in the elevation and a wider sector (4°) in azimuth. This narrow fan-shaped beam then is nodded up and down in an arc from about 2° to 32°. The other characteristics of this radar include PW of 2 to 3 microseconds, and PRFs of 200 to 400 pulses per second, with an effective range of about 200 nm. The RF is again above 2,500 mHz so that the beam may be shaped into its characteristic pattern.

Ground Controlled Intercept—uses the combined information from the EW and HF radars which provide azimuth and elevation, and a double check of range. A site having both an EW and HF radar has a three-dimensional fix on a target and can thus vector an interceptor into the area.

"V" Beam—derives its name from the shape of its transmitted beam. Two fan-shaped beams similar to that of the EW radar beam are swept concurrently. One beam is vertical and the other is at some convenient angle. In addtion to range and azimuth from the vertical beam, a time difference between intercept echoes from the two beams on a target tells how far up the "V" the target is. This provides altitude information.

Direct Threat:

Gunlayer (GL)—is a relatively low-powered, precision radar using conical scan for tracking and either helical or spiral scan for acquisition. In conical scanning, the radar beam is made to describe the shave of a cone in space. The apex of this cone is located on the antenna and the angle of the cone is less than twice the width of the radar beam normally radiated. A target within the constraints of the beamed energy sends back a constant amplitude echo from all beams and the radar thus is said to be "locked-on" the target. If the target moves out of the area of overlap, returns of varying amplitude are sent back to the radar as the beam rotates through one complete cycle. A comparison of signal strengths creates an error signal and causes the antenna drive unit to move the antenna in the direction of the strongest return.

To isolate one target and increase the speed of gathering data, the conical scanning radar usually operates with a high PRF (1,000 to 2,000 PPS), narrow PW (0.5 to 1.5 microseconds), and highlights the target with its pencil beam. A complete set of azimuth and elevation data is received by the radar every revolution of the beam (approximately 1,800 rpm). This means that the maximum rate of gathering data is about 30 times per second. The RF is usually between 2,500 and 3,000 mHz to facilitate beam-shaping. The actual beam width can be reduced to less than 2° with an effective beam width less than 1/2°.

The small beam width of conical scan makes it ideal for tracking but relatively useless for acquiring the target. Using a helical or a spiral search pattern allows a large area to be searched with a pencil beam. As soon as the target is found, the radar transitions into the conical scanning track-mode. As a point of interest, transition time can be reduced by the use of a Palmer scan (the superimposition of conical scan onto one of the acquisition scans).

Airborne Intercept Radar (AI)—uses conical scan or monopulse for its tracking mode and either raster or spiral scan for target acquisition. Actually, the only difference between the conical scan used for AI operation and gunlayer operation is the RF. An airborne interceptor radar system usually operates above 8,500 mHz to reduce the physical size of the transmitter and receiver components.

The acquisition scan is necessary since the GCI resolution cell is so large. The spiral scan pattern is the same for gunlaying and airborne interceptors. Raster scan serves the same purpose as spiral scan and differs primarily in the scanning pattern. Palmer scan may be used to decrease transition time.

Surface-to-Air Missile Radar (SAM)—consists primarily of monopulse and track-while-scan systems. The monopulse system obtains sufficient information from each transmitted pulse to update its computers and reposition its antenna. Instead of scanning a single beam, the radar uses a minimum of four separate beams which transmit together but receive independently. By comparison of the energy returned in the beams, azimuth and elevation corrections can be made. The two advantages of this system over conical scan are its speed in gathering data and its ability to track a target even though there is a large amount of pulse-to-pulse fading.

The basic operation of the airborne monopulse radar is identical to the SAM's; however, details are changed to make the system compatible with the over-all airborne weapons system.

Track-While-Scan (TWS)—is not a tracking radar in the usual sense. It produces two beams; an elevation sectoring beam and an azimuth sectoring beam. It is analogous to operating a collocated precision height-finder and air-surveillance radar. Each beam sectors a fixed quadrant and has the capability of displaying several targets simultaneously. The PRF usually is above 1,000 PPS and the sector rate is approximately 16 Hz. Updated azimuth and elevation data are obtained with each sector of the two beams. Since the antenna does not "highlight" the target, the system is unaffected by pulse fading.

Non-Threat:

Over-the-Horizon (OTH)—is principally employed as a missile launch detection system. By using an RF energy scatter system, the OTH radar can detect ionospheric disturbances caused by missile penetration.

Airborne Navigation—are high-frequency systems (above 8,500 mHz) that give a pictorial display of the territory below the aircraft. When used in conjunction with an associated computer, Doppler radar and astrotracker, the airborne navigation system is extremely accurate and reliable.

Side-Looking (SL or also Side-Looking Airborne Radar—SLAR)—are mapping radars that use the zero Doppler shift abeam the aircraft to create an extremely small "artificial aperture" (synthetic aperture). The radar returns are printed on film in rasters very similar to television. These rasters produce a continuous "strip photograph" of the area abeam the aircraft.

Space Surveillance (SS)—are low frequency radars (UHF band) with pulse widths in excess of 2,000 microseconds and peak power levels in excess of three megaWatts. To obtain the necessary accuracy, antenna diameters of 25 ft. are common. These radars can detect targets with a one-square-meter cross section out to 2,000 nm.

Air Surveillance (ASR)—are associated with most airports. Typically, the ASR is used for departure and approach control and as an acquisition radar for ground control approach. It is a relatively precise, short-range radar. PWs normally are less than one microsecond and PRFs are in excess of 1,000 pulses per second. Sweep rates are usually 12 to 20 rpm. Range is on the order of 50 to 90 nm. Frequencies of operation usually are between 2,700 and 2,900 mHz.

FINAL NOTES:

The following has been extracted from the remarks of the late Ben R. Rich during the F-117A final delivery ceremony on July 12, 1990:

"Prior to program go-ahead, five dedicated air staff officers reporting to Gen. Al Slay, clearly

Two F-117As, No. 831 (left) and 783, just prior to being placed on show at the Edwards AFB open house during October of 1993. F-117As have become relatively commonplace static displays at U.S. airshows, though physical contact with the aircraft remains forbidden due to RAM technological sensitivity and RAM fragility.

defined a set of top level requirements for the F-117 weapons system. Then, a system program office (SPO) with a minimum number of people was established at the Aeronautical Systems Division, under direction of the late Gen. Dave Englund (then a Col.). Similarly, a small Lockheed team was also established under the leadership of Norm Nelson. The F-117 SPO and Lockheed Program Office were supported by other organizations and groups whose efforts were crucial to the program. These included the Air Force Office of Special Investigations which developed and implemented effective security procedures; the Air Force Logistics Command's Sacramento Air Logistics Center which provided secure, specialized logistics support including supply support; and the Tactical Air Command which worked closely with Lockheed and the SPO to initially define operational requirements and later establish a secure, full operational and maintenance capability at the Tonopah Test Range Airfield.

"Working together, this F-117A team established streamlined management methods wi~h clear lines of communication and regularly scheduled meetings, but with a minimum amount of formal reporting. An appropriate amount of oversight was provided, but the team was not overburdened. We created a non-adversarial, problem solving environment built on trust and commitment. Together, we guided the program through development and production and into operational service while maintaining the highest standards of program security.

"As a result, the F-117 was developed and fielded in record time for a modern fighter aircraft. Only 31 months after go-ahead, on June 18, 1981, Lockheed test pilot Hal Farley flew the F-117 for the first time. And with concurrent development and production, initial operational capability was achieved only 28 months later, during October of 1 983.

"We built the F-117 at two a season, or 8 airplanes per year, and achieved a 78 learning curve. The Skunk Works guaranteed range, radar cross section, and bombing accuracy. All guarantees were met."

Companies whose participation in the F-117 program has been declassified include:

Allied Signal Aerospace Co. of Torrance, CA: auxiliary power system; emergency power system; environmental control system; and air data transducer.

American Fuel Cells Coated Fabric Co. of Magnolia, AR: fuel cells.

Delco Electronics of Goleta, GA: digital tape set 1553 computer and lab support equipment.

Explosive Technology of Fairfield, CA: formable explosive charges for tailhook cover.

F. L. Aerospace, Grimes Div. of Urbana, OH: sccondary cockpit lighting; inflight refueling lights; and electroluminescent panels.

General Electric Co. of Binghampton, NY: engines; fuel quantity system; engine performance indicator; engine signal detector unit; and generator.

Goodyear Tire and Rubber Co. of Akron, OH: tires.

GTT Industries, Inc. of Westlake Village, CA: hardware/software for PC-based automated test system.

Harris Corp. of Melbourne, FL: digital moving map radar and digital tactical/display system.

Hitco of Gardena, CA: (no product listed).

Honeywell, Inc. of St. Petersburg, FL: radar altimeter inertial navigation system; air data computer; and color multipurpose display system.

Two F-117As have been painted in special markings. The first bore a stylized U.S. flag on its undersurface, and the second carried the special LADC skunk in recognition of the retirement of Skunk Works immortal, Ben Rich.

IBM of Oswego, NY: mission computer.

Kaiser Electronics of San Jose, CA: projection interface unit (PIU) and projection display unit (PDU).

Lear Astronic Corp. of Santa Monica, CA: flight control computer/navigation interface and autopilot computer (NIAC) system.

Link Flight Simulation Corp. of Binghampton, NY: weapons system trainers and software for simulator.

Lockheed Aeronautical Systems Co. of Ontario, CA: mobile training unit.

Loral Aircraft Braklng System of Akron OH: brakes wheels, and anti-skid brake control system.

Lucas Aerospace Power Transmisslon Corp. of Utica, NY: power transmission shaft.

Menasco of Burbank, CA: main landing gear and nose landing gear.

Natlonal Waterllft Division of Pneumo Corp. of Kalamasoo, MI: servo actuators.

Northrop Corp. of Norwood, MA: rate gyro.

Parker-Hannifin Corp. of Irvine, CA: fuel system values.

Pioneer Aerospace Corp. of S. Windsor, CT: parachute system.

Sargent Controls of Yorba Linda, CA: contro. (throttle) and switch matrix.

SCI Technology, Inc. of Hunstsville, AL: data bus coupler.

Serracin/Sylmar Corp. of Sylmar, CA: windshield panels.

SLI Avionic Systems Corp. of Grand Rapids, MI: expanded data transfer system and altitude heading reference system.

Sundstrand Corp. of Rockford, IL: air turbine starter.

Teledyne Controls of W. Los Angeles, CA: annunciator panel.

Western Gear Corp. of City of Industry, CA: aircraft mounted accessory drive gearbox (AMAD).

XAR Industries of City of Industry, CA:

inflight refueling valve.

ACRONYMS & ABBREVIATIONS:

AAA	anti-aircraft artillery
ACES	advanced capability ejection seat
ADP	advanced development projects
ADRAM	advanced radar absorbent material
AI	airborne intercept
ALCM	air-launched cruise missile
AM	amplitude modulation
ASR	air surveillance radar
ASV	air-to-surface vessel
CRT	cathode ray tube
DARPA	defense advanced research projects agency
dB	decibel
DECM	defensive electronic countermeasures
DLIR	downward-looking infrared
ECM	electronic countermeasures
EW	early warning/electronic warfare
FLIR	forward looking infrared
FM	frequency modulated
FM-CW	frequency modulation/continuous wave
FSD	full-scale development
GCI	ground control intercept
GHz	gigahertz
GL	gunlayer
HARP	Halper anti-radar paint
HF	height finder/high frequency
Hz	Hertz
IR	infrared
IRAM	improved radar absorbent material
IRCM	infrared countermeasures
kW	kilowatt
LRR	long range radar
MHz	megaHertz
nm	nautical mile
OTH	over-the-horizon
Pavg	average power
PPI	plan position indicator
Ppk	peak power
PRF	pulse repetition frequency
PRT	pulse recurrence time
PW	pulse width
Radar	radio detecting and ranging
RCS	radar cross section
RF	radio frequency
RHI	range height indicator
SALT	strategic arms limitation talks
SAM	surface-to-air missile
SLAR	side-looking airborne radar
SS	space surveillance
TWS	track-while-scan
UHF	ultra-high-frequency

Because of its size, the F-117A sits relatively high off the ground. This particular aircraft 828, flown by 37th TFW commander Col. Tony Tolin, was used during the unveiling of the type at Nellis AFB, and one week later, also was flown to Carswell AFB in Ft. Worth, Texas for an airshow.

The F-117's wing leading edge is extremely sharp—which is unusual for an essentially subsonic aircraft. It is, however, optimized for RCS rather than aerodynamic considerations. Visible in this view is the left-side dorsal radar reflector as well as the flattened, "platypus"-type exhaust nozzle.

Size of elevon and flap assemblies, which take up most of wing trailing edge, is readily apparent. Elevons control both pitch and roll. When the aircraft is "powered down", these surfaces tend to droop to their full-trailing-edge-down position as a result of hydraulic pressure bleed.

IN DETAIL:

Tony Landis

Jay Miller/Aerofax, Inc.

Primary cockpit multifunction displays (MFDs) consist of two medium-sized side units and one large central unit. HUD is centrally located above instrument panel and center MFD.

Canopy RCS details include angled plates on forward edge of canopy frame and on various transparency frame edges. Canopy is hydraulically raised and lowered.

Tony Landis

Jay Miller/Aerofax, Inc.

Cockpit interior is fairly conventional. ACES II ejection seat, contrary to generally circulated information, is standard medium gray. Panel combing is black.

Canopy peak is faired light for illuminating dorsally-mounted inflight refueling receptacle during night operations. There are three locking latches on each side of canopy.

Jay Miller/Aerofax, Inc.

When closed, canopy fits snugly except where dog tooth edges overlap primary structure to prevent radar energy from penetrating and reflecting. FLIR unit fits underneath gold-colored screen just ahead of windscreen. FLIR and laser designator unit rotate into position when activated. Screen permits energy out, but not in.

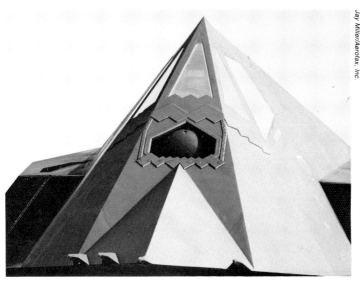

Dome-like FLIR/laser unit is readily visible behind protective, non-reflective screen. Screen apparently is quite fragile and must be replaced with significant regularity.

Canopy framework, like rest of aircraft, is covered with RAM. Basic premise of canopy was to reduce radar return from cockpit, which historically is one of the best reflectors.

Special segmented boarding ladder has been developed to ingress and egress the F-117A. Noteworthy is protection provided on wing leading edge and cockpit railing.

Nose flat-plating is particularly pronounced. Noteworthy is the fact that there is no conventional boundary layer bleed system between fuselage side panels and intakes. Prism effect is considerably less pronounced under nose, but is considerably more linear. There is no leading edge break from nose to wingtips.

Four pitot-like assemblies feed environmental data to quadruple redundant fly-by-wire flight control system and instrumentation. Pitot assemblies are composite construction and apparently have been difficult to heat for deicing purposes. Diamond cross-section is the end product of RCS detailing.

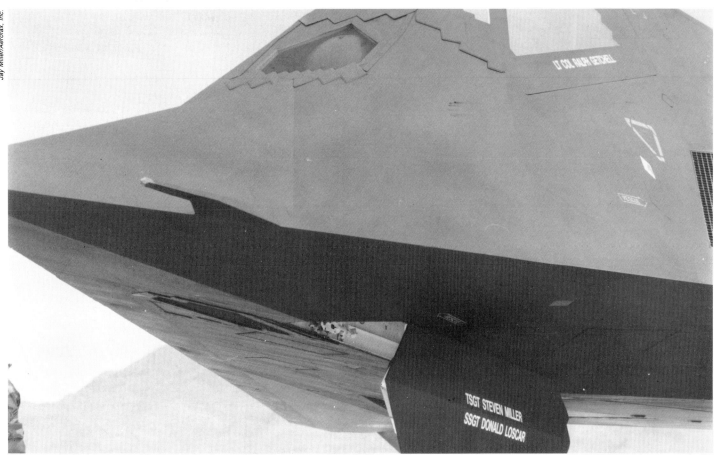

Centerline node begins at extreme tip of nose and continues to point under fuselage where it contacts flat plate area. Node then breaks and sets up nodes for first wing flat plate section forward of main spar. Geometry of design is extremely complex and is the result of work conducted utilizing a Cray computer.

A total of four pitot assembles (three are visible here) are mounted assymetrically on nose leading edge section. Two pitot tubes protrude from the starboard leading edge, one is mounted on the extreme tip of the aircraft nose, and a single fourth pitot is mounted on the port leading edge.

Nose tetrahedron assembly has sharp edges. Section is faired into flat plate into general cockpit area inside of which is mounted the FLIR/laser unit. The latter projects its energy through a gold-colored screen/mesh which some sources claim to be elastic. Screen/mesh is easily damaged by rain, insects and related objects.

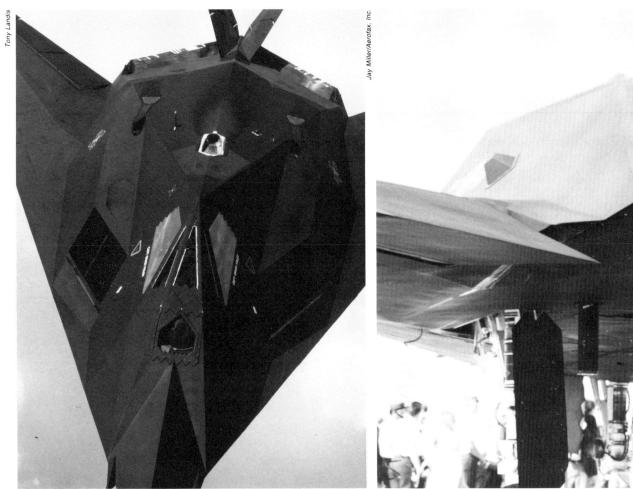

Jay Miller/Aerofax, Inc.

Tony Landis

Jay Miller/Aerofax, Inc.

Downward Looking Infrared (DLIR) unit is mounted on underside of fuselage, just starboard of the nose landing gear well. This unit also apparently contains a laser designator assembly similar to that mounted in the upper FLIR compartment. Like the upper unit, the DLIR covering is a translucent gold-colored screen.

Rotatable FLIR turret, mounted in recessed bay just ahead of windscreen, has three optical viewing ports with the left side port being the largest.

Trailing edge root extension is concession to inward angling of engine compartment flat plate area. Noteworthy is triangular piece projecting from exhaust lip extension.

39

Because the F-117A is optimized to provide an absolutely minimal radar return, it is often equipped with special radar reflectors on each engine compartment flat-plate, just above the wing root. These are easily removed and their mounting holes then can be filled with spray-on RAM. Photos show variations to mounting area.

Aft section of aircraft and wing assembly present minimum cross-sectional area. Position of national insignia, unit badge, and radar reflector are readily discernible. Wing appears to have a thickness/chord ratio comparable to other contemporary attack aircraft such as the Vought A-7 "Corsair II".

Wingtip has interesting faceting arrangement which results in broadening taper to sharp edges. Where plates meet, however, there is some rounding of corners. Extreme tip, however, is very pointed. It is possible to mount a removable night-flying light on the wingtip if needed.

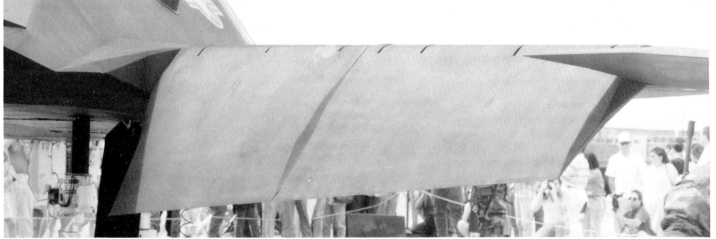

F-117A is equipped with both elevons (outboard) and flaperons. Both units are hydraulically boosted (thus the sag when the aircraft is powered-down). Faceting is carried through on inboard and outboard edges of these surfaces. Flaperons have three sealed hinge points, and elevons have four.

Wing leading edge is perfectly straight with no visible cap breaks. Slab surfaces meet at equally linear node lines. In cross section, wing has a hexagonal airfoil. Wings are wet with integral fuel tanks. All control surface and flap gaps are tightly sealed. Structure is primarily aluminum.

Detail view of RAM application to V-tail assembly. Vertical surfaces have unusual double-diamond airfoil section in consideration of RCS requirements. Actuation of all-moving portions is hydraulic. Moving surfaces are rudders and serve to input yaw moments only through F-16-type rudder pedals in cockpit.

V-tail is the first of the its kind on any operational manned combat aircraft in the U.S. Construction is presently aluminum with external RAM covering.

View looking forward between V-tail surfaces. Visible under extreme aft section of empennage are what appear to be viewing ports for aircraft RHAW system.

Nose landing gear is hydraulically steerable. Last three digits of aircraft serial number are in red.

Nose gear retracts forward and gear well door closes in concert. Door has separate hydraulic unit to ensure tight fit after closing. Nose gear is hydraulically steerable. Tire size is 22 x 6.6-10.

TSGT STEVEN MILLER
SSGT DONALD LOSCAR

Nose gear door has serrated rear edge. Noteworthy is node line down door center. Visible on port side of door is access panel for external power and communication.

Main gear well forward door assembly is equipped with a shallow indentation to accommodate oversized wheel and tire. Bulge can be seen externally in the form of prism.

Main landing gear are equipped with Goodyear 32 x 8.8 26-ply tubeless tires. Aft door assembly cover is attached to gear strut at an angle to conform to retraction cycle. Forward door assembly is hydraulically boosted.

Main gear strut assembly is extremely rugged to accommodate heavy aircraft payloads.

Main landing gear retract forward via hydraulically-actuated scissor assembly. Right main gear well accommodates single-point refueling receptacle.

Original main gear brake assemblies were prone to fire following hot and heavy landings. Tube-like device on right is bolt-on radar reflector.

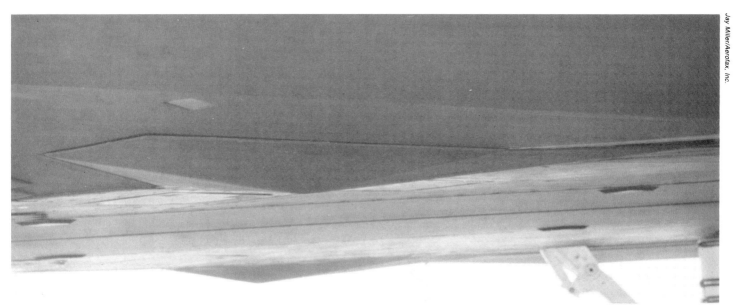

Forward section of gear well doors can be closed when the aircraft is on the ground. Their prism-like shape serves to cover bulge of oversized main gear wheel and tire assembly. Relatively tight fit is apparent. Main gear well door consists of two parts. Aft section is affixed to main gear strut.

Starboard intake screen. Screen is designed to reduce to negligible numbers the radar return normally generated by the engine compressor section face. Because of the screens, radar energy can only enter and return from directly in front of the aircraft. All other energy is dissipated long before it is reflected.

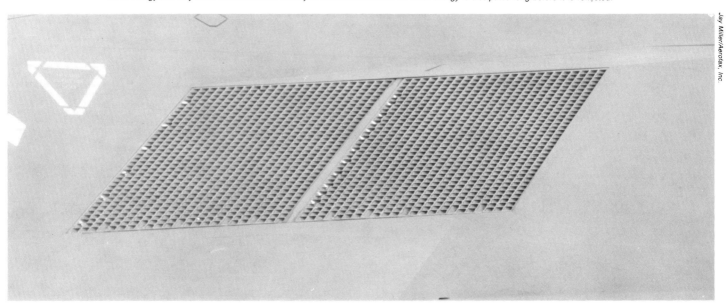

Port intake screen. Intake size is considerably larger than General Electric F404 requirements normally would dictate. This serves to compensate for the restricted intake flow caused by the screens. Noteworthy are slot dimensional variations at screen base, probably due to attachment devices.

When viewed from almost head-on, intake screen virtually disappears, underscoring its minimal effect on intake airflow. Stepped lower intake lip contains mechanical wiper/scraper mechanism for physically removing ice upon pilot command. Large duct area is conventional without S-curves.

General Electric F404-GE-F1D2 turbofan engines utilized in the F-117A are quite similar to the McDonnell Douglas F/A-18's F404-GE-400 with the exception of the afterburner. The latter is deleted from the F-117A's engine and there are apparently dedicated modifications that enhance the engine's low-observable characteristics.

General Electric F404-GE-F1D2 engines are representative of state-of-the-art low bypass turbofan technology. Visible are power take-off units with associated oil and hydraulic pump assemblies. Exhaust nozzle arrangement differs considerably from afterburner-equipped F404s.

Aft view of F-117A reveals how completely exhaust nozzles are shielded from low-attitude observation. Upswept empennage section considerably reduces exposure of hot exhaust nozzles to infrared sensors. Upper surface of lip is thoroughly insulated with "Space Shuttle"-type tiles to absorb heat.

Exhaust nozzles are flattened at the aft end of a large plenum into which the F404s eject their hot exhaust gases. Plenum serves as mixing point for cooler bypass air sucked in through slots just ahead of and beneath intakes. Coupled with ambient air mixed after passing over top of aircraft, the final exhaust efflux is relatively cool.

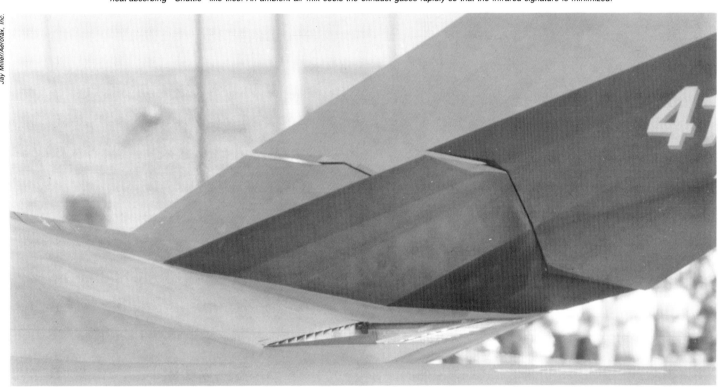

Flattened exhaust nozzles are divided into twelve exhaust slots. Gases exiting these impinge on the extended lower lip of the flattened empennage section which is covered with heat-absorbing "Shuttle"-like tiles. An ambient air mix cools the exhaust gases rapidly so that the infrared signature is minimized.

Flattened exhaust nozzles are only about six inches deep. In being recessed behind extended empennage lip, the infrared signature from anywhere beneath the aircraft is reduced to absolutely minimal values. Thrust degradation is minimized by providing greater cross-sectional area and minimizing obstructions in the plenum.

Upturned empennage trailing edge lip probably provides some aerodynamic input due to its shape. Though appearing rounded, it is, in fact, faceted like the rest of the aircraft. Ground level observation of the exhaust nozzles is restricted by the lip assembly as it stands over seven feet.

Jay Miller/Aerofax, Inc.

Bomb bay doors consist of two separate units which are hydraulically opened and closed. Hinge attachment points have multi-faceted covers. There appear to be two separate bays for weapons. Up to 5,000 lbs. of ordnance can be carried. Rectangular mark in foreground outlines tailhook enclosure.

Tony Landis
Tony Landis

Wing tip, flap, and elevon faceting conforms to node lines of main wing panels and is very pronounced. Night formation light on top of wing tip is recessed in consideration of RCS.

In order to facilitate inflight refueling at night, the apex of the canopy frame serves as a mounting point for an inflight refueling receptacle illumination light.